NOTES FROM A TRAVELING CHILDHOOD

Readings for Internationally Mobile Parents and Children

A Foreign Service Youth Foundation Publication
Karen Curnow McCluskey, Editor

TABLE OF CONTENTS

FOREWORD

The Foreign Service Youth Foundation (FSYF), established in July 1989, is a private, non-profit "umbrella" organization which coordinates the efforts of groups interested in supporting American Foreign Service youth around the world, develops programming for the benefit of Foreign Service young people, and ensures funds for these projects.

The Foundation evolved from the recommendations of the "Youth Project Committee" convened by the Family Liaison Office of the State Department with participants from the Association of American Foreign Service Women, the Overseas Briefing Center at the Foreign Service Institute, and the Medical Division of the Department of State.

Although the Foundation focuses its efforts on assisting the children of employees of the foreign affairs agencies of the U.S. government, many of the experiences of those children are familiar to the children of military, international business, missionary and academic families with overseas assignments.

The Foundation works closely with the Department of State and other agencies to provide a "flow of care" for Foreign Service youth from the Washington, D.C. area to overseas posts and back again. One component of that "flow of care" is Around the World in a Lifetime (AWAL). AWAL, a program established ten years ago by teens and their parents, provides social activities for teens (and sometimes their parents) as they reenter the United States or prepare to go overseas. Since its inception, AWAL has expanded into a year-round cycle of activities, including a teen-produced monthly newsletter (Wings of AWAL), videotapes and T-shirts, internships, and contacts with Foreign Service families overseas.

In addition to its work with teens, the Foundation sponsors informative programs for parents about raising internationally mobile children. Presenters include education and mental health professionals, as well as experienced Foreign Service parents and young people. It also sponsors the annual Foreign Service Youth awards, which honor the community service contributions of Foreign Service youth both in the United States and abroad.

The Foundation is currently exploring an expansion of its programs to include younger children and young adults. With this volume, it is venturing into the field of publications as a vehicle for broader dissemination of information about growing up internationally.

In this book, we have tried to gather writings that bring to life that exciting and challenging experience we call "Foreign Service," and offer some insights into ways that you and your family can get the most from it. We hope you will find it helpful.

We welcome your comments and your questions about our activities. For more information about the Foundation, please write us at:

Foreign Service Youth Foundation
P.O. Box 39185
Washington, D.C. 20016.

We wish you joy in your journeyings.

Betty W. Atherton
President and Chairman of the Board

June 1994

ACKNOWLEDGEMENTS

The editor and the members of the FSYF Publication Committee would like to thank all those who helped make this book possible, including:

The Interviewees (individually listed on page 34), who shared their experiences, suggestions, and memories so candidly,

The Family Liaison Office for their support of this endeavor at every stage,

The Office of Overseas Schools of the U.S. Department of State, which provided much helpful information and guidance,

The Office of Medical Services of the Department of State, especially Elmore Rigamer and Billie Wilds, for providing significant background materials and support,

The Overseas Briefing Center at the National Foreign Affairs Training Center (Department of State), especially Sheri Mestan Bochantin, for supplying a wealth of materials on internationally mobile children,

Norma McCaig of Global Nomads, for sharing the unique perspective of the many global nomads she represents,

The parents and children who have succeeded from whom we can learn how to manage and delight in an internationally mobile lifestyle, especially those who have shared their thoughts and experiences in the articles that appear in this book.

A WORD FROM THE EDITOR

During my interviews and reading about the subject of parenting internationally mobile children, I was struck by the tremendous insights of parents, children, and health and education professionals.

So many of the interviewees spoke with great emotion, from their core, to get across the intensity of their convictions. You can see this same intensity of emotion in many of the articles in the latter half of this book. I expected a far deeper divergence in the perspectives and experiences of the different communities and sub-cultures that I explored. In most cases, what I got instead were different twists on the same themes.

I was astonished by the eloquence of the children who have grown up internationally; I see a fraction of that eloquence in my work as a trainer. I was equally surprised by the maturity of these young global nomads, and by the willingness of children and parents to disclose not only the delights, but also the drawbacks of international parenting.

The commitment of all involved in this project to create a candid publication that didn't whitewash the sometimes complex issues of parenting internationally was refreshing. Although in some cases specific examples are camouflaged to ensure confidentiality, this book tries to present the emotions, the difficulties, and the joys of parenting internationally.

This book would not have been possible without the patience and support of my husband Tom or without the living lessons of my two temporarily-rooted daughters, Meghan and Allison, who have brought me perspective and who have taught me the true essentials of effective parenting.

Karen Curnow McCluskey

INTRODUCTION

"Raising children is a creative endeavor, an art rather than a science," Dr. Bruno Bettelheim says in his text, *A Good Enough Parent.* "I cannot tell the reader how to experience this art, or how to appreciate what is involved in it, for these are far too personal matters to be decided by others, although [other's] views about [parenting] may enhance our ability to perform creatively, in our very own ways..." (Bettelheim, page 14).

In this book you won't find cookie-cutter solutions that can be applied across-the-board to all children. The basic premise of the book is that you can't approach parenting with a rigid set of rules or techniques that will work in all situations for all children. What you will find are issues other parents have faced and strategies they have used to raise children successfully in an international context.

This book is broken into three parts. The first overview article presents information gleaned from a literature review and from interviews with parents, children, mental health professionals and educators. The second and largest section of the book includes both previously published and never before published articles by children and parents who have experienced international moves, as well as articles by education and mental health professionals who work in this area. The final section of the book contains an annotated bibliography of additional resources on the topic of international parenting.

THE EXPATRIATE PARENT:
Issues and Options for Internationally Mobile Parents

by Karen Curnow McCluskey

Introduction

The myriad of parenting books that line bookstore shelves is proof that parenting can be a herculean responsibility wherever you are located. Parents who place this responsibility in an internationally mobile context face additional challenges and complexities.

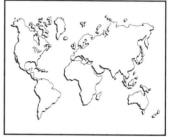

How do parents who move internationally manage? What problems do they face? What do their children take away from the experience? Are these children better or worse off than their geographically-rooted peers? *Notes from a Traveling Childhood* begins to answer these questions.

This overview article combines the opinions of health and education professionals with the real-life experiences of internationally mobile parents and children. The articles, books, and interviews that formed the basis for this article raised some interesting and sometimes disturbing issues that parents and children face when moving and living outside of their own country. They also uncovered some of the tremendous advantages -- what some call the edge -- these parents and children have because of their international experiences.

****

The Internationally Mobile Lifestyle

The community of people who move from and live outside of their home country for extended periods of time is significant in number. It includes businesspeople, missionaries, government employees, military personnel, and staff from international organizations such as the United

Nations and the World Bank. This expatriate community also includes family members of these employees. The effects of international moves can be both wonderful and difficult for all who move, but the impact can be especially hard-hitting for children. Since many of us did not grow up in an internationally mobile environment, we may often wonder if how we manage the international moves and adjustments with our children is effective. Even those of us who did grow up internationally may stumble through unknown territory since the realities of international living and working have changed.

****

What Mom Never Told You

> *We all bring to our children what our parents gave to us. That's really very good. But, there has to be some modification of that.... Parents of any time have to confront things that their own parents didn't. You have to take this international lifestyle into account when you're talking about how to parent these children.*
> Dr. Elmore Rigamer, Director, Office of Medical Services, U.S. Department of State

Continuous and fast-paced change, increasingly a part of all our lives, further complicates the job of parenting. As one parenting authority comments, "Even those of us who were fortunate enough to have had warm, loving, competent parenting find that our parents' methods aren't always adequate to meet the pressures of our complex, changing society, with its conflicting values and overwhelming choices.

Changes are occurring at such a fast pace, we find ourselves preparing our children for a world about which we can only speculate" (Shiff, page xx).

Internationally mobile families face even more change, even more transitions than do most families who are geographically stable. Parenting internationally brings with it its own set of issues, problems, and opportunities -- some of which are true for parents anywhere, some of which are specific to the internationally mobile lifestyle.

Dr. Elmore Rigamer, Medical Services Director for the U.S. State Department, comments, "You *should* bring [to your parenting approach] what your mother and father did. That's not bad. But there are some things you're going to have to do differently if you are raising children overseas. You have to add to what your parents did for you. [One of the most important elements you must add] is recognizing your children's individual responses to moves so you know how to manage them, discipline them, encourage them."

HEALTHY PARENT: HEALTHY CHILD

Cross-Cultural Adaptation

The cross-cultural adjustment to a new country required of employee and family member alike is fraught with challenges and exciting new opportunities often not present in the same way in the passport or home country. Parents face the task of not only making their own adjustment successful, but also easing their children's adaptation to the new school and home environment. The impact of the parents' own adjustment process on the children can be tremendous.

The cultures international employees and their families encounter in international assignments include not only the host country culture, but also the international expatriate community culture, the culture of expatriates from their home country, the culture of the sponsoring organization in that location, and others. Each of these cultures and sub-cultures has its own set of mores and assumptions; each one also requires an adjustment.

For most adults and children, the cross-cultural adjustment process does not happen overnight. Rather, it is a process, a series of stages that require varying lengths of time depending on the characteristics and personalities of the individuals involved, other issues the family is dealing with at the time, prior international experiences, and many other factors.

David Pollock, cross-cultural expert and Executive Director of Interaction, Inc., describes five stages of transition: *involvement* (characterized by a sense of belonging and intimacy), *leaving* (marked by celebration, distancing and denial), the *transition* itself (identified by chaos, anxiety, and lack of status), *entering* (distinguished by superficiality, marginality, and vulnerability), and finally, *reinvolvement* (defined by a return to a sense of belonging and intimacy).

****

The Last One on the List

As parents, we experience our own process of adjustment, with all the pain of leave-taking, the chaos of arriving, the anxiety of not belonging, and finally the relief of adjusting, of reaching some point of equilibrium. At the same time, our children are going through a similar transition. Making sure we take care of ourselves in our own adjustment is crucial, both to serve as a role model of adjustment skills for our children and to refill and re-energize ourselves so that we can help our children move through their adjustment process.

In an international setting, taking care of ourselves means: being aware of our own process of adjustment, knowing our signs of stress, and using the stress management techniques that work best for us. (See inset on page 7, *International Stress Management Techniques*.)

Often as parents, we become so focused on caring for our children that we neglect ourselves, putting our needs and feelings last on the list of things to consider. Knowing where you are in the adjustment process and being patient with yourself as you adjust to your new setting can help you maintain perspective in good times and bad. Denying your own needs in the transition process is not only unhealthy for you, but unhealthy for other family members, too.

International Stress Management Techniques
(Karen Curnow McCluskey)

1. *Know thyself.* Understand what causes stress for you, how you respond to stress, and which stress reducers work for you.

2. *Take control.* Develop long and short term goals that are realistic and attainable in an international setting.

3. *Eat healthy, exercise, and be merry.* Live a healthy lifestyle. Maintain a good sense of humor about yourself and about the many mistakes you may make in adjusting to the new culture.

4. *Avoid stress like the plague* by managing your time effectively. Set priorities, alternate fun and challenging activities, plan for crises, communicate and behave assertively.

5. *Know when it's time to slow down.*

6. *Use good cross-cultural communication skills.* Get to know your new home by reading, making friends with "cultural informants," learning the language, and getting out.

7. *Say no.* When the demands of everyday life get to be too much, decline invitations, decrease activities, give yourself a "refill" break.

8. *Take care of yourself.* Recognize your own reactions to the adjustment process and respond as you would to anyone else: provide the support and resources you need. Practice relaxation techniques. Get involved in activities that you enjoy.

9. *Take care of your family.* Help minimize your family's stress by listening, hugging, understanding, being there. Your own stress will be better managed as a result.

10. *Don't try to eliminate stress completely.* Stressors are a natural part of life, although we certainly get more than our quota in an international lifestyle. Offer and encourage lots of love and support among family members during stressful times.

In *Experts Advise Parents: A Guide to Raising Loving, Responsible Children*, Eileen Shiff says, "...Total self-denial drains the parent and the parent-child relationship. In demonstrating healthy self-respect you gain the respect of your children. Learn to balance the needs of all family members, including your own. In addition to reducing your stress, you're teaching your child the art of cooperation, compromise, and sensitivity to others' needs as well as his own. Those skills will be valuable to him in future relationships."

Adjustments and transitions don't happen in a vacuum. In addition to understanding where you are in the adjustment process, it is important to take into account other issues the family may be facing at the time of the move. Elderly or ill relatives, the loss of a loved one, divorce, whether the family has moved internationally before or not, and other family crises and situations are life stage issues that can dramatically affect a family member's ability to adjust to a foreign culture.

****

Role Changes

In addition to these cultural adjustments, employees and their family members also face role changes. Employees may encounter the increased stress of becoming the primary or sole bread winners for the first time. Employees may also find their work responsibilities have changed, possibly requiring high visibility, high risk duties and longer working hours. In addition, they may be required to do more work-related entertaining than is customary in their home culture, further increasing their work hours.

The accompanying spouse may have a change in employment status -- often to at least short-term unemployment -- and may have difficulties adjusting to this change in role and position within the family. The children no longer have the same activities or friends to turn to and may need to develop new abilities and interests to relieve boredom and grow. The frequent result of all these changes for family members is closer family ties and a more insular family structure -- with all the benefits and pitfalls that come with it.

ORGANIZATIONAL SUB-CULTURES:
THE IMPACT OF AFFILIATION

The occupational affiliation of an expatriate can also affect how parent and child adjust and develop. The length of an assignment and the nature of the "business" of the sponsoring organization can both influence the view expatriates have of the host culture and their perceptions of how difficult or easy the adjustment will be.

****

The Tour of Duty

For many people, the length of an assignment to a foreign country seems to have a great impact on the adjustments of adults and children. At one end of the spectrum you have contractors and certain military employees who are at post for a short period of time (for a year or less) and others, such as most U.S. Defense Attachés, who may serve in only one overseas assignment before returning to their home countries.

At the other end of the time continuum, you find many missionaries and certain countries' foreign service personnel who may stay 10, 20 years or more in the same location. Most business and diplomatic corps personnel are somewhere in between the two extremes. For example, many businesses keep their staff in one location for five or six years; the U.S. Foreign Service rotates their employees every two to three years. The length of a tour can affect an employee's or a family member's entire approach to a new culture and may influence the development of children.

The Short Term Sojourner

People who are assigned to a foreign country for a brief tour of duty, which may or may not lead to another international assignment, may never get out of a tourist mentality in approaching the host culture. Children's development may not be affected as dramatically as it is with individuals who stay outside of their home country longer. For this group, the posting is an adventure, one which perhaps is kept short to avoid adverse affects on the employee's career progression. Children in this setting seem to adjust fairly well on the whole, although it is not completely free of difficulties. This short-term scenario can be particularly difficult for the high schooler, especially if the tour comes during the last two years of high school.

The Transients

> *Not only did I grow up overseas, but my whole life was transplanted every two or three years to a place with different soil, different sunlight, and different rainfall. By the time I settled in, unpacked, made friends, and found roots, it was time to move again. Growing up is tough for everyone, but I had to do it on the move.*
> Michael Featherstone, son of
> U.S. Foreign Service Officer

Many organizations, like the U.S. Foreign Service and many businesses, assign employees to a specific international location for two to six years per tour. People in this setting often do multiple tours successively before returning to their passport country. As is evident in the above quotation, adjustments for children and  adults in this situation is decidedly different from that of the short term sojourners described above.

Connie Buford, Executive Director of the Association of International Schools in Africa, has observed the impact of the more frequent moves on children. She comments, "The foreign service child and the business child are similar in that often they both realize that their assignments are temporary. These children tend not to make lifelong friends because they know they'll be leaving, that they've done this before. The result may be a feeling of resentment toward parents." Norma McCaig describes this phenomenon as a "set up camp, break camp" mentality. As mentioned in the section, *Adolescence: Coming of Age*, not all parents agree. Some believe that the friendships their children have made internationally will be longer lasting than others.

Since people in this category may stay overseas for long periods of time (albeit in a variety of locations), children may attend various schools in an international school system for their entire education, raising concerns about college preparedness and reentry (adjustment back to the home culture after an extended period overseas). Dr. Rigamer believes children in this category face some of the greatest challenges since the "issues that threaten the most stem from continuous changes in relationships and dealing with feelings of loss and depression that result when there is no thread of continuity."

Those In It For The Long Haul

Missionaries, some foreign service corps and some private sector companies choose to send their staff to one location for long periods of time, sometimes sending the employee to one location for most, if not all, of a career.

While these families may not face the issues of upheaval and loss normally associated with more frequent moves, they nonetheless have to learn to deal with frequent transitions and change, as they see good friends moving in and out of their lives every few years. In some ways, this may be even more difficult than having to make the change.

While relating some of her childhood experiences as the daughter of an internationally mobile pharmaceutical executive, Norma McCaig, now Director of Global Nomads International, says: "Yes, it's true that the two or three year scenario really does have to be managed differently. But, to put in a word for folks like myself who lived in capital cities for longer periods of time, the experience we had was people cycling in and out of our lives every two or three years. As part of the expatriate community, those who are rooted for a longer period of time are still exposed to very high turnover. There is something very painful about the dynamic of being left, because you don't have the excitement to help you through the transition."

Norma's internationally mobile childhood has spurred her to create and direct an organization committed to assisting and validating the culture and experiences of what Norma calls "global nomads," people who have lived abroad before adulthood because of a parent's occupation.

In his *Descriptive Statements of Missionary Families,* Clyde Austin, Chair of the Psychology and Intercultural Studies program at Abilene Christian University, describes some of the unique characteristics of missionary families, who are typically in one overseas location for a very long time. Compared with other expatriate families, Dr. Austin comments that missionary families often have: better preparedness for cross-cultural living, a stronger desire to live overseas based on the family's mission, greater dependence on the local economy, lower family income, a better command of the local language, a greater sense of divided loyalty between the host country and home country, and possibly greater social constriction due to geographical isolation.

****

The Nature of the "Business"

The kind of organization and the type of product or service it provides, also has an impact on family members -- adults and children alike. In addition to adjusting to the cultures they come in contact with overseas, families face other issues that are a direct result of the "business" of the sponsoring organization.

For military and diplomatic corps families, children may feel they are supposed to represent their country -- a task that may be difficult if the child has been overseas a long time, carrying the flag all these years of a country in which he or she may have spent very little time (and then only as a tourist for periods of home leave or between postings). Missionary children may share this sense of "representational responsibility" because of the nature of their parent's occupation -- and societal or local expectations of them.

A common concern of military and foreign service families is security. Bobbie Jones, Attaché Support Officer with the Defense Intelligence Agency, comments, "One reason military families are concerned about security is the service member is a very obvious target.... The service members do wear their uniforms, not a suit or short-sleeved shirt that would help them blend in so as not to be pinpointed as an official representative [of their country]."

Increased social demands placed on many internationally mobile employees, such as increased expectations for entertaining, may also affect children's development. One parent speculated that this increase in the amount of entertaining responsibility was one reason internationally mobile children develop social skills and a comfort in communicating with adults so much faster than their geographically-rooted counterparts.

Expatriate employees enjoy varying amounts of support from their sponsoring organizations. Business community employees and family members overseas are often left to fend for themselves on the local economy, in many cases enjoying fewer of the home country amenities sometimes afforded to diplomatic and military officials through commissaries. As one education official commented, the business employees may, however, receive allowances (such as more frequent trips home) not afforded to diplomatic and military families. The types and amounts of job benefits provided to employees can affect their adjustment to an overseas environment.

Bob Sills, Director of the Rabat American School, notes, "sometimes problems arise because of expectations families have of the level of support they will receive [from the sponsoring organization]." These expectations may not be fulfilled since benefits may and often do vary from one post to another.

Another source of difficulty may come from the assignment systems of the sponsoring organizations and how much input the employee has in the posting decision. Many of the most disgruntled employees seem to be those who are posted to a country they have not chosen and where they don't want to be. Troubled or disgruntled parents may very well pass their negative outlooks on to their children, possibly increasing the difficulties the children have in adjusting to their new environment.

INTERNATIONAL PARENTING ISSUES THAT CROSS CULTURES AND SUB-CULTURES

What do your parents give you that is eternal, that goes across cultures? Good common sense, a love of children, a sensitivity to the needs of children, and a belief that your children's needs should be considered along with your own. That's a very tall order, especially given the needs of children today.

Dr. Elmore Rigamer

Children face certain issues at different times in their lives, regardless of geographic location. Internationally mobile children confront some common challenges -- no matter what their occupational affiliation. While certainly not comprehensive, the following discussion highlights some of the most common issues that internationally mobile parents may encounter with children of different ages.

****

Babies, Toddlers, and Preschoolers: Home Is Where the Parents Are

Since parents serve as the primary anchors for these age groups, most interviewees agreed that this was the easiest time to move children internationally. Young children also tend to have fewer ties outside the home than older children. International parent Bobbie Jones comments, "Kids who are not yet in school are the easiest to deal with [in an internationally mobile lifestyle]. When you've got a babe in arms, it's relatively easy to travel together... It's when the child reaches the point where their life is not home [that other adjustment issues begin to crop up.]"

Nonetheless, parents need to address some of the strong needs these young children have. While for parents this may seem like an easy time to move children, if the move is not managed well, it may have negative effects on young children.

Anne-Marie Atkinson, clinical social worker and global nomad comments, "Toddlers, like teens, are fiercely involved in a drive for independence and, at the same time, a need for dependence. They depend on routine and sameness for much of their sense of security. Compared with older children, they are limited in their ability to understand and comfort themselves during the upheaval of a move."

Since the parents or other familiar caregiver are so important to these

children, Dr. Rigamer advises parents to avoid dropping young children off with strangers, especially during the early days of an overseas assignment. Dr. Rigamer also suggests that establishing a routine to maximize the amount of predictability in the now unpredictable lives of these youngsters and making sure they have their favorite toys are both great helps during international moves. Parents also need to be attentive at the end of a posting, when a young child may feel sadness at leaving a beloved nanny.

****

Middle Childhood: The Importance of "Stuff"

Saying goodbye to their "stuff" and their house seemed to present some of the greatest difficulties for school-aged children not yet in their teens. Since children in this age group focus on what is here and now, when their" stuff" is packed in boxes, from their perspective, they may not see it again for a long time, if ever. For this reason packing out is a tough time in the transition process for these children.

Another difficult time comes immediately after arrival at post. This age child may not yet have the self-confidence to walk up to a child he or she does not know and make friends. Parents report that it is far easier if you arrive when school is in session because activities are already set up for students. If you arrive in the summer time, it is important for the parent to help these children get out into the environment and find a friend, particularly if the child doesn't yet speak the language or if the housing is spaced far apart. Anne-Marie Atkinson suggests, "Skills and peer acceptance are very important to

children in this age group in forming their self-concepts and sense of self-esteem. Parents can help by encouraging the development of transferable skills and abilities."

Children in this age group may also begin to develop real friendships with other children, making separations even tougher. Their sense of national identity also begins to form during this time. Nonetheless, Dr. Rigamer comments, "children in this age group are still fairly adaptable and flexible. They may not reject a new culture or language and may pick up a new life fairly easily."

****

Adolescence: Coming of Age

Most of the interviewees agreed that adolescents face some of the greatest difficulties in the international move process. In the video, *Raising Children Abroad*, Dr. Rigamer comments, "Teens rebel. They find everything difficult, in part because of the developmental tasks that they must accomplish: separating from the family and gaining their personal identity.... Kids return to the bosom of the family, which is great for family unity, but he/she is not separating him/herself and asserting him/herself or becoming more autonomous. You can really see here how the developmental process becomes a real yo-yo in a mobile lifestyle. A step forward and a step back."

In her book, *The Foreign Service Teenager At Home in the U.S.: A Few Thoughts for Parents Returning with Teenagers*, Kay Branaman Eakin describes the special impact moves have on teens. "One of the reasons transition.... has such a strong impact on adolescents is that they are going through the greatest changes in growth and development of their lifetimes. The acceptance of their bodily changes and.... the establishment of good relationships with members of the opposite sex is a confusing task for many young people. Even in the most stable of environments, adolescence is often a traumatic time, both for the teenager and the parents.

Moving is an emotion-filled period in which teens must give up old friends, worry about whether they'll like their new school and whether they'll ever be able to find new friends.... It looks pretty ominous -- new home, new school, no friends. They usually do end up making new friends and fitting into their new life, but it may take much longer than expected, and in the meantime, they may be pretty unhappy." (Eakin, page 3)

Richard Johnson, an international representative of Goodyear who has raised two children internationally, outlines another aspect of international life that affects adolescents. "Sports," Johnson remarks, "are not always terribly organized in overseas locations. The resources are not always available to be able to play sports [in the same way that we might in our home country.] On the other hand, the sports activities that are available are often less competitive, allowing more children the opportunity to play."

There are other distinct disadvantages for teens in this lifestyle. Connie Buford identifies two rites of passage that geographically-rooted U.S. teens experience that internationally mobile children don't. These rites of passage may apply to other nationalities as well. The first rite of passage is the driver's license. U.S.-based teens get their driver's license earlier than most internationally mobile teens can. This license issue has been the source of awkwardness for many teens returning to the U.S. for college. The second rite of passage is work. U.S.-based teens begin working at a much younger age, thereby becoming acquainted with the world of work at a younger age, seeing a wider array of professional role models, and having their own spending money. While internationally mobile teens may develop independence in other ways, the freedom and independence that comes from these two rites of passage are often not possible for internationally mobile teens.

One parent raised a concern about her child's ability to plan ahead. "I find that my daughter and some of her international friends are reluctant to make plans too far ahead, which is a big problem with getting into college. They always figure there's a new change coming. They don't want to make too many firm plans just in case things change."

Parents disagree on the effect international living has on their children's ability to make friends. One parent commented that the friends her children made "will be their friends forever, whether they correspond or not. They'll probably be better friends than the ones they meet here in the U.S. because they went through some times together overseas that are difficult." Another parent observed superficiality in friendships, especially among the more transient children.

EDUCATING OUR MOBILE CHILDREN

The Choices

One of the greatest concerns parents have when facing an international move is, "What schooling will be available to my child? Will my child be disadvantaged academically as a result of this move?" Although this fear is certainly strongest in families moving overseas for the first time, even the most seasoned, who may experience somewhat less stress since they "know the ropes" of international schooling, often have concerns about their children's education.

Dr. Ernest Mannino, Director of the State Department's Office of Overseas Schools, and Dr. Keith Miller, Deputy Director of the office, spoke candidly about some of the common concerns parents have regarding the education of their children. Dr. Mannino and Dr. Miller caution parents against making assumptions about their children's education, even if they have served in other international locations. To make an educated choice, parents need to think through schooling issues and to research post schools as far in advance of a move as possible.

Since each posting offers different educational options, new choices will need to be made and an adjustment will need to take place in each new location. If children have special needs of any kind, appropriate schooling options overseas may be limited and therefore must be researched carefully.

Children who are internationally mobile have many choices of schools to attend. In most major cities, there are schools based on the U.S., French, German, and British systems. Some parents also opt to become their children's teachers through home schooling. Which school is appropriate for your child is an individual decision based on many factors.

One of the primary factors that should be considered, according to Dr. Mannino, is what type of college or university your child will attend after high school. "Some parents want an international education, not just an education within an American system school," Dr. Mannino points out, "and fortunately, they have the opportunity to go to these types of schools." Dr. Mannino goes on to say that what parents must keep in mind is "Will this school best prepare my child for education beyond high school?"

Parents may be tempted to alternate their children's school system in order to enhance cross-cultural understanding and tolerance, but many experts advocate just the opposite. Mannino and Miller warn that differences in the sequencing of curriculum do exist in the high school grades; moving your child from one academic system to another during this time (for example, from the British to the French or the U.S. systems) can handicap a child academically. At the very least, the parent should learn what the differences in curriculum are and, to the extent possible, keep the child in one system (although this may be in more than one location) for all of the high school years. Dr. Rigamer applies this recommendation to all grades, not just high school. He advises, "It's clear that whatever continuity you can provide these children is important. The nice thing about the American school system or the French, German or whichever, is that it's the *same* school system throughout their lives, throughout a life in which there are many other changes."

Many parents are hoping their children will matriculate into a college or university in their home country. Especially in the high school years, it is important to select the school system that will best prepare your child for the college of choice and stick with that system throughout the high school years.

Other factors that affect school choice include: your child's grade, language skills, and personality, as well as the length of your assignment. Dr. Rigamer maintains that, despite some parents' desires to have their children learn other languages through their schooling option, most children will want to go to the school that has other children from their passport culture. He goes on to say that, "You don't have to do what your children want all the time, but if your daughter really isn't making it [in a foreign system school] -- and I think a year is more than enough time -- I would really rethink, *'Whose needs am I really satisfying?'* Do you want a trilingual neurotic or a very healthy monolinguist?"

****

The Benefits

The international school systems offer considerable benefits to the mobile child. Unlike less transient students in domestic schools, students in international schools have a tremendous sense of empathy for new kids since almost everyone has been new at one time or another. There is also increased opportunity and access to athletic teams and unique international activities (for example, "model congress" and "model U.N." activities) than may be available domestically. Many of the international schools have excellent academic standards. The Office of Overseas Schools reports that graduates of the  approximately 190 schools it assists achieve SAT scores well above the national average. These children also often make it into excellent universities, in part because of their international schooling. As Dr. Miller comments, "If a child has been overseas and has a good academic standing, he or she may well win out over another college applicant with an equally good academic record, but no overseas experience."

****

Recommendations

Dr. Mannino and Dr. Miller provide the following recommendations to parents:

> ### Making International Schooling Work
> (Dr. Ernest Mannino and Dr. Keith Miller)
>
> *Research before selecting.* Physically visit all the schools available to you so you can make an informed decision about which school your child will attend. Although their suggestions and comments may be useful, don't go solely on the advice of anyone at post. Find out what programs are available and make a choice that best suits you and your youngster.
>
> *Get involved.* Meet the teacher(s); attend parents' night; get involved with the PTA; whenever possible, get involved on the school board.
>
> *Maintain close contacts with the school.* Don't wait until you have problems to make a connection with the school. If problems do arise, handle them immediately where the problem is. For example, if the problem is with a teacher, approach the teacher and discuss a strategy to solve the problem.
>
> *Meet with Office of Overseas Schools personnel* when they visit your post to provide them with relevant information and to ask for their assistance.

UNIQUE PARENTING CHALLENGES: DUAL CULTURE MARRIAGES AND SINGLE PARENTING

Dual Culture Marriages

Dual culture marriages are not uncommon among expatriate communities. These families face the unique challenge of multiculturalism within the home as well as in the environment in which they live. Like children who are raised outside of their passport country, foreign-born spouses are often called upon to represent a culture about which they have only a tourist understanding.

Children in intercultural marriages have first-hand, personal experiences with a myriad of customs and assumptions; their development is directly affected by this mix of cultures. In *Intercultural Marriage: Promises and Pitfalls*, Dugan Romano identifies many issues that intercultural couples must face, which run the gamut from differences in the very basics such as food and eating habits, to discrepancies that exist with more complex issues such as religion, male-female roles, political views, and concepts of child-rearing.

One of the tough issues of dual culture marriages revolves around language. Problems may arise for children who have limited abilities with the dominant language of the school they are attending. Bob Sills of the American School in Rabat comments that the non-English speaking children in his school have by far the hardest time. Other complications may arise for dual culture marriages where the parents speak different native languages. The decision of which language the children should learn is often well thought-out and deeply felt, evidenced by one dual-culture marriage parent who burst into tears as she described the thought-process that went into her family's decision.

In *The Moving Experience: A Practical Guide to Psychological Survival*, Gail Meltzer and Elaine Grandjean offer the following advice for cross-cultural marriages, "Remember, you and your partner are two separate people. Accept the fact that you can have two sets of needs and expectations. Separate external conflicts from internal ones and work to reduce or eliminate each on its own." Meltzer and Grandjean encourage dual culture couples to communicate openly, by asking questions whenever uncertainties arise, instead of trying to guess or mind read what the other person is thinking.

****

Single Parents

Single parents face unique challenges when moving children overseas. If the single parent is divorced and parent-child relations are healthy, making extra efforts (and possibly spending additional money) to ensure that contact is maintained with the absent parent is in everyone's best interest. This contact helps the single parent contend with any tendency his or her child might have to idealize the absent parent and helps to maintain some balance in perspective and role modeling for the child.

International families can become, as one writer put it, "highly nuclearized," possibly resulting in greater dependency on the family. In the case of the single parent, this can go both ways: greater dependency of the child on the single parent and greater dependency of the single parent on the child. Connie Buford, an internationally mobile single parent comments, "As is true sometimes for the stay-at-home spouse when the employee travels or for single parents, adults can't expect children to entertain them. Grown-ups need to look for their own entertainment."

Health professionals and single parents who have successfully managed overseas assignments offer the following suggestions. Arrive at post as early as you can. Work out with your office how to balance the double-pull of being on the job right after arrival at post and of being with your child during the transition. Educate your office and the new school about single parenting issues. Be aware that there may be a lot of resentment from your fellow employees that you have special needs and might get special consideration. Get other stable, consistent relationships in your child's life.

Parenting author Eileen Shiff comments, "Single parents have even greater need for renewal. With their increased responsibilities and diminished adult support, they often report that they feel as though they are 'running on empty.'... Some parents try to fill the space of the missing parent by trying to be both mother and father to their child. It is not practical for the parent, or in the best interest of the child, to try to assume both roles. Instead, provide opportunities for [your child] to interact with consistent role models of the opposite sex. Above all, when you think you can't possibly do it all, don't! Set priorities." (Shiff, page xviii.)

A SENSE OF ROOTS

Parents, children, and education and mental health professionals disagreed most strongly on the issue of what Norma McCaig calls "cultural confirmation." On one end of the spectrum are those who believe that parents must provide a cultural identity for their children based primarily on the parents' home culture. At the other end are those who believe just as strongly that an exclusive insistence on the parents' home culture in fact invalidates and devalues the multicultural nature of internationally mobile youth.

One of the things we must provide for our children, the first group contends, is our own cultural foundation. Connie Buford comments "Make sure you give kids a sense of roots for stability. If asked where they are from, they can answer 'Cleveland' [or some other definite location]. This is very important."

Dr. Rigamer agrees. "A sense of roots," he states, "a sense of connection with the extended family and the home culture are all very important. You cannot give these up. The children really need to be rooted or grounded in their home culture. They need to spend time with their extended family. This means that instead of staying in Europe for an R&R, you should come home. Later on the children can become citizens of the world by spending that summer in Tibet or French language studies in France instead of coming to Louisville, Kentucky. The former more glamorous, the latter much more important in terms of psychological health."

Dr. Rigamer goes on to say, "There's no such thing as the international child. That's a label we apply. But a child has to have a sense of where she's from, where she belongs, who her people are, what her culture is, what her beliefs are, before she can open up and become international. You have to have something to start with before you can take everything in.... If you're a citizen of the world, you're a citizen of nowhere."

On the other side of the argument, there are many global nomads who take great pride in being "a citizen of the world" and feeling a connection to and responsibility for the people of more than one country. Anne-Marie Atkinson calls this the "no man is an island" point of view, and suggests that in an increasingly interdependent world this is a useful and positive point of view to have.

Some believe that an exclusive or very strong focus on raising a child in their parents' culture may be confusing and frustrating for children. Norma McCaig maintains, "Early on there needs to be a recognition of the fact that the children are going to be of a different culture than the parent.... The parents are inculcated with the values and mores and assumptions of the passport culture and they have an international overlay, whereas the children who grow up in one or more countries are enculturated in that international culture.... [This means that sometimes, when parents are returning to their passport culture], the parents may be *returning* home, but the children are *leaving* home.... Children from this environment will never be totally U.S. American or Ugandan or Malian, never totally of that passport country. They will never be monocultural. This is more of an asset than a liability in today's world."

Supporters of this view state that children are more influenced by the local culture than are their parents, since they are in a state of formation, with their minds wide open. Parents, therefore, must provide support and flexibility, not rigid insistence on their own culture, as children start wrestling with the issue of cultural identity. According to this view, the greatest casualty of an exclusive insistence on the parents' culture is the child's self-esteem. If parents have rigid expectations of their children being monocultural like them, what the child internalizes is a lack of worth for and lack of affirmation of their multicultural identity.

"Nonetheless," Norma McCaig adds, "some rooting is important, with the understanding that the global nomad root system is more relational than it is geographical.... The reason I kept going back to reunions of my high school in India was these people were my home town. Alternate thinking is required for the whole idea of establishing a root base."

THE GIFTS WE GIVE:
MOBILIZING OUR MOBILE CHILDREN FOR LIFE

What Our Children Gain

What do the children who move internationally during childhood gain from the experience? What do they leave with that might make them different from geographically stable youth? The written research on the impact of international living on children is inconsistent at best. Despite other differences in perspective, many of the people who were interviewed for this publication do agree on some fundamental traits that internationally mobile children tend to develop because of their international experiences.

Deep Understanding and Tolerance for Differences

The constant exchange with a myriad of cultures may encourage a deeper tolerance for and acceptance of differences among people. Richard Johnson observes, "These children have no strong prejudices." "I do not think these children," Dr. Rigamer adds, "are as quick to think in racial stereotypes as children who live in one place." Connie Buford offers an explanation, "Since they have friends from all over the world, they are more tolerant, more open, kinder. Overseas, you can't have status symbols like clothes because you can't get them here, so kids are more tolerant of the way people look."

A Broader Vision

Richard Johnson describes how his children and others he has observed sometimes walk away with some wonderful values that are not in the mainstream of the passport country, for example, the strong family values of Latin America. Connie Buford adds, "These children have a greater sense of the world than they would have otherwise... The world of the future is going to be a small one. Our kids have the advantage: they know how to travel, they know the world. They hit their freshman year of college and see their U.S.-based counterparts as less mature.... [Children who have lived in one place] often have worlds that are so much smaller."

Comfort Communicating with Adults

A striking characteristic noted by every interviewee was the difference between internationally mobile children and geographically-rooted children in how they converse with adults. Most international children, interviewees commented, are very much at ease at a dinner party with adults. They are more sophisticated in the best sense of the word and seem to have more confidence with adults.

Commitment to Community or Social Service

"Especially if they have served in third world countries, our children," Connie Buford notes, "will have a value toward social or community service." The internationally mobile child seems to have a greater sense of the need to help the needy, a trait perhaps encouraged by the international school systems overseas, most of which are involved in some community service activities.

Closer Family Ties

Every interviewee spent considerable time talking about the increased focus on family ties. "Families are much closer since there are not as many peer distractions as you might have [in your home country]," Richard Johnson states.

Norma McCaig explains, "Since the family is the only consistent unit that moves through time and place, the family members are thrown back on one another in a way that they are not in a geographically rooted situation. They become far more dependent on one another -- practically and psychologically. This can have very positive implications, but it can also mean that any dysfunction that exists is exacerbated because of  the intense emotional involvement of family members. They don't have the same safety valves or resources (such as other relatives or close friends to take the children for short periods) for dealing with these problems."

Richard Johnson comments, "These kids are comfortable anywhere. They like a diverse environment around them. They have friends of all kinds from all different cultures. In fact, some of them may be uncomfortable with a homogeneous group.... For the job market 2000, we need staff who will be flexible and comfortable anywhere. It will be important that they be able to learn quickly and be flexible. These internationally mobile kids have a leg up in this respect."

****

Suggestions from the "Experts:" Parenting Strategies That Work

The similarities in interviewees' suggested parenting strategies were remarkable. Despite differences in organizational affiliation, many of the same approaches and techniques for managing internationally mobile children were echoed by parents, educators, and health professionals. Norma McCaig highlights what she sees as the most important issues international parents face in her *Five Cs for Parenting the Internationally Mobile Child* (see inset, page 31). In her *Parenting Internationally: Tools You Can Give Your Mobile Children to Help Them Thrive* (see page 86), Anne-Marie Atkinson outlines some essentials for the international parent. Other recommendations from people who have "been there" are provided below.

☑ *Prepare, prepare, prepare.* The success of a transition to a new country is very strongly, although not exclusively, linked to how much the family prepares for their new posting.

Bobbie Jones comments, "People who do more preparation seem to be more successful, seem to do better. Sometimes families who have moved internationally before don't do as much research on their next assignment. This is a big mistake. It's never the same in the next place. You need to do the same amount of research even before coming back to the States as you did going out."

Richard Johnson recommends that employees and family members read pre-departure materials carefully, since every country is different. He comments, "Among other things, find out about what you can buy and what you can't. Consider not only what you deem important or necessary, but also what your children might find important."

Some specific recommendations on how to prepare include: visit or get a video or pictures from people of the post; get information from Embassies; visit a travel agent and get all the handouts you can on the country; go to the library and get books on your country of assignment (even for small children, stories about where you are going may help with their adjustment); learn some phrases in the language before you get there; take advantage of any office that provides family support for your organization.

 Include children in the planning of the move. Start option-giving as early as possible, even when children are very young. One internationally mobile mother comments, "If you're moving to a brand new bedroom for a toddler and his or her favorite color is purple, then maybe you should bring a purple rug. It's only for two or three years, so who cares? And if it grants the child a sense of security, consistency, or control, it is well worth it. What to sell, what types of clothing to buy before you go, what color the child's bedroom will be, what to bring to put in that bedroom, are all opportunities where parents might allow children input on the changes that are coming."

Parents must be clear, however, about what they will accept in their children's choices before they give children the right to make a decision. One military child was very pointed about this when she said, "Don't ask me to make a choice, and then change your mind on what I decided. It's not fair."

 Recreate "home." Connie Buford advises, "Bring things like posters and stuffed animals with you. Keep the kids' rooms the same. The pictures on the wall may get thread-bare, but drag them around anyway."

 Say goodbye. Children who were evacuated out of a posting before having the chance to say goodbye report that those feelings of "unfinished business" stay with them for a long time. David Pollock comments that those feelings may stay with them for life. Be sure to use whatever closure techniques are important to your child.

 Look on the positive side without being phoney. Children will reflect what you feel. Focus on the positive, on the new adventure you're going to have. As one parent said, "Try not to lay your own 'stuff' on your kid." Dr. Mannino adds, "Tell your children as much as you can in an age-appropriate way. Don't transfer to your children unnecessary concerns or worries. Perhaps the result of a closer family unit, certain concerns get raised that might not otherwise." Dr. Rigamer advises parents and children, "Move into your new society with energy and non-judgementally."

 Realize the impact of the adjustment process. Whereas it is important to approach the move positively, parents need to realize that all will be experiencing an adjustment process that will have its ups and downs. Richard Johnson comments, "Prepare yourself for a tough first six months. The early months in any new location involves a lot of adjustments." Connie Buford adds, "Parents need to be supportive and realize the adjustment. Be sensitive to the things that may seem silly, like phone calls, posters, whatever."

In the video, *Raising Children Abroad*, Dr. Rigamer urges, "Let [your children] talk about their emotions and allow them to feel sad. Show them that you not only understand how they feel, but that you too have these feelings of sadness and regret." When your children are showing signs of stress, support them where they are. As Anne-Marie Atkinson comments, "Families are, after all, a place to share both joy and sorrow."

 Help children make and keep friends. Make sure kids interact and get to know one another. Encourage children to keep in touch with the friends left behind.

 Keep an eye on grades. Parents need to stay attuned to their children's education. If lower grades persist beyond six months at a new post, Dr. Rigamer cautions, "you may want to consult with a teacher or a counselor to make sure there are not deeper problems. It may be the move, but it could be something else surfacing."

Norma McCaig's Five Cs
for Parenting the Internationally Mobile Child

Communication: Communicate with your children as non-judgementally as possible, encouraging them to express their emotions freely, rather than denying them. Maintain the relationship with your child by resolving conflict through honest dialogue.

Continuity: Provide as many constants for your children as you can in this discontinuous lifestyle (e.g., moving family furniture and maintaining personal family rituals from country to country). Predictability is very important and can serve to get children excited about the lifestyle.

Collaboration: Involve children in decision-making to the extent that you can. (For example, allow them to make choices of what items will be packed and which ones will be stored.) Give kids as many choices as you can.

Closure: Make sure your children have adequate time to say goodbye to people and things as you are leaving one location and moving to another. According to David Pollock, in this lifestyle, goodbyes are often "multiple, simultaneous and intense." If denial of the transition is encouraged, strong, unaddressed emotions can leave a child with a sense of loneliness and unresolved grief.

Cultural Confirmation: Affirm the value of the multi- or bi-cultural nature of your children. They cannot be monocultural in the way that someone raised in your passport country will be. Reflect on your own values and why you hold them. Make an honest assessment of your own biases before judging the behaviors of your global nomad children.

Establish reasonable guidelines, limits, and rules within which your children must stay no matter where you are. Norma McCaig comments, "Global nomads need parental consistency."

In *Raising Children Abroad,* Dr. Rigamer adds, "This is especially important for adolescents who are in a period of experimentation anyway. A common situation that crops up in this regard is international teens located in a culture that is tolerant of alcohol and drug use at an early age." One way Dr. Rigamer recommends that parents deal with this situation is to say something like, "It's fine for these people to do that, but in our country [and/or in our family], we don't do it that way." Joel Wallach and Gale Metcalf's article, *Safe Kids, Involved Parents* (see page 92), provides additional suggestions on community-based limit setting.

 Know when you shouldn't go. If you have the choice, take an inventory of the issues the family is facing before agreeing to take on an overseas assignment. Dr. Rigamer recommends that children not leave during their last two years of high school when they are subject to both social and academic pressures. Richard Johnson adds, "Think about who should go. Make sure there is a sense of adventure and a strong willingness to see new things."

In Summary

Parenting is a challenging art, especially in view of the rapidly changing, shrinking world in which we live. Internationally mobile parents have to be especially attuned to the needs of their mobile children, focusing on all of the developmental requirements for different ages, just as their geographically rooted counterparts do.

Internationally mobile parents have additional complexities that they must manage, including adjusting themselves to the new cultures they enter, easing their children's cross-cultural adjustments, nurturing cultural identity and roots for their children, and operating in new roles and under different rules than their parents did. The most successful international parents are those who recognize, understand, and respond to their children's individual reactions to moves, who listen to and selectively follow the advice of those who have "been there," and who

TIPS FROM KIDS TO KIDS

Parents can learn a lot by listening to kids speak with kids. The children who served as resources for this book offered the following recommendations for other children in an internationally mobile lifestyle.

Eat the food *from the country where you are being posted. If the waiters and waitresses are from that country, watch how they behave, and perhaps try out some of your language skills on them.*

Get a pen pal. *Write to the school or to your office at your new assignment to get names and addresses of other kids who might serve as pen pals.*

Be careful because your parents go crazy. *One child comments, "I know that when we get ready to pack out, my mom gets meaner than a snake. I'm prepared for that."*

Watch out because your parents will forget important things, *like where the keys or tickets are. Take some responsibility for remembering, in order to make up for your parents' forgetfulness.*

Say goodbye, *but make sure you don't shut the doors of where you are prematurely. Be sure to say goodbye to the kids at school, to relatives, to the babysitter, to your friends. Have your friends sign an autograph book.*

prepare thoroughly before embarking on any international endeavor, including the one that brings them home.

The task of international parenting can be overwhelming. As Rosalind Kalb and Penelope Welch state in *Moving Your Family Overseas,* "through it all, we have the opportunity to watch our children grow in unique ways.... Children develop a sense of themselves and the world that is truly special.... They feel a part of the places they have been and the places become a part of them."

Taking stock of the unique qualities of our internationally mobile children, we see that many children who have grown up internationally mobile develop a deep understanding and tolerance for differences, a broader world view, comfort in dealing with new situations and with adults, a commitment to community or social service, and close family ties -- qualities that will serve them well in our increasingly diverse world.

ENDNOTES

Interviews for this article were conducted in March and April, 1994 with the following people:

Elmore Rigamer, Director of the Office of Medical Services, U.S. Department of State; Norma McCaig, Director, Global Nomads International; Bobbie Jones, Attaché Support Officer, Defense Intelligence Agency, and all the children and adults she surveyed; Clyde Austin, Chair of the Psychology and Intercultural Studies program, Abilene Christian University; Connie Buford, Executive Director of the Association of International Schools in Africa; Richard Johnson, international manager for Goodyear; Kay Branaman Eakin, Education Counselor, Family Liaison Office, U.S. Department of State; Sharon and Michael Featherstone, U.S. Foreign Service mother and son; David Pollock, Executive Director of Interaction, Inc.; Ernest Mannino, Director, and Keith Miller, Deputy Director, U.S. Department of State, Office of Overseas Schools; Anne-Marie Atkinson, LCSW-C, clinical social worker; and Robert Sills, Director, Rabat American School, Rabat, Morocco.

In addition, text references in this article were derived from the following books, documents, and video- and audio-cassettes.

Austin, Clyde N. *Descriptive Statements of Missionary Families.* Abilene, Texas: Clyde N. Austin, 1986.

Bettelheim, Bruno. *A Good Enough Parent: A Book on Childrearing.* New York: Alfred A. Knopf, 1987.

Eakin, Kay Branaman. *The Foreign Service Teenager -- At Home in the U.S.: A Few Thoughts for Parents Returning with Teenagers.* Washington, D.C.: Overseas Briefing Center/Foreign Service Institute, Department of State, 1988.

Kalb, Rosalind and Welch, Penelope. *Moving Your Family Overseas.* Yarmouth, Maine: Intercultural Press, Inc., 1992.

Meltzer, Gail and Grandjean, Elaine. *The Moving Experience: A Practical Guide to Psychological Survival.* Philadelphia, Pennsylvania: Multilingual Matters Ltd., 1989.

Pollock, David C. *The Transition Model.* Albany, NY: Interaction, Inc., 1990.

Raising Children Abroad. Washington, D.C.: Video produced by the Department of State's Family Liaison Office, Office of Overseas Schools, and Office of Security Awareness, 1993.

Romano, Dugan. *Intercultural Marriage: Promises and Pitfalls.* Yarmouth, Maine: Intercultural Press, 1988.

Shiff, Eileen. *Experts Advise Parents: A Guide to Raising Loving, Responsible Children.* New York: Delacorte Press, 1987.

PORTRAITS OF THE TRAVELERS

Someone once said, "Nothing speaks louder than experience." The following series of articles chronicles the many experiences of parents, children, mental health professionals, educators, and researchers who have lived or studied issues that internationally mobile families face.

From the classic cross-cultural research of Useem and Downie to the heart-felt impressions of 13 year-old Edward Finn, in these writings you will view firsthand accounts of people who have "been there."

In the unique perspectives, insights, intense emotions, and reassuring suggestions found in these readings, we hope you will gain new cross-cultural competencies, increased awareness, and encouragement to help you and your family prepare for your own internationally mobile life.

LONGING FOR AMERICA:
Notes from a Traveling Childhood

by Sara Mansfield Taber

I have been resting on my futon eating donuts and reading memoirs. This has been my mid-afternoon treat, before picking up my daughter at school, since my family and I moved from St. Paul to Washington last summer. The memoirs are those of people who grew up in places like the Bronx and St. Paul--rich memoirs thick with the creams and sausages and pastries of family lives deep-fried in a specific tradition and culture. As I read of the Czech grandmother's cellar full of fermenting sauerkraut and beets, of her garden of dillweed and rhubarb, and of the soft skin of her kissed cheek, my body floods, to the tips of my fingers and toes, with the ache of loss. My childhood as the daughter of a globe-trotting C.I.A. officer does not fit into the aspic mold of the American memoirs I have been gobbling of late.

In place of the girl sitting combed and eager at Grandmother's Sunday dinner in St. Paul or The Bronx, I offer a girl who was born amid the rancid smells of Japanese fish markets, who raced her brother over the rainy hillocks of Dutch dunelands, and who earned the beginnings of adult consciousness during a summer of visiting the stump-fingered residents of a Bornean leper colony. Magic dwelt in these places of Europe and Asia--there is an elixir that trickles through one's body while tramping for the first time the alley of a strange country, when licking an odd-tasting ice cream drawn from cows fed on unfamiliar grasses, and upon seeing new varieties of trash in the gutter--but there was, in this girl, the one without the Grandmother and the Sunday dinners, an ever-present sense of homelessness, and more, a deep and burning longing. The longing for America.

In A Romantic Education, Patricia Hampl writes of snoozing in a St. Paul kitchen on Sunday afternoons, after having stuffed herself with Grandmother's pork roast and hot buttered carrots. The woman from that medium-size city in America's bosomlands explains the full meaning of her mid-afternoon sleep. "But something sweet and starry was in the kitchen and I lay down beside it, my stomach full, warm, so safe that I'll live the rest of my life off the fat of that vast family security."

When my eyes pass over Hampl's words--in spite of savory memories of scores of varied, exotic meals that I sampled during my child years--I am seared freshly by the pain of connective tissue ripped from my heart and irrevocably lost.

In another passage, Hampl describes her reverence upon watching the adults in her extended family hand around glasses of the first dandelion wine of the season. The scene, of known and dear adults sharing the family's home-concocted spirits, has a hallowed glow.

I can frame no family rhythms analogous to those of Hampl. I have no American home nested within an identifiable culture, no extended family, with time-seasoned rituals carried forward through the generations with the regularity of the arrival of day. In my family there was none of the cleaving to tradition that I read of in so many memoirs. My upbringing provided no fixed point, no firm, inviolate behavioral code to respond to, carry forth, or rebel against. My family's tradition, rather, was to vary our customs year by year. At Christmas time, in countries oceans distant from my parents' families, we celebrated eagerly, putting out the few tree ornaments we shipped from place to place, but mainly adopting the festive practices of the country in which we had landed. In Holland, we celebrated Sinter Klaas on December 6th. Following the example of our Dutch friends, we wrote funny poems that spoofed our friends' habits, and then dashed around town, leaving them, unsigned, on our friends' doorsteps. In Borneo we decorated a potted palm with tiny Iban baskets, and sweated in our good clothes while we opened gifts on the veranda among the orchids.

In one hand, I treasure each odd and idiosyncratic Christmas. Each memory suffuses a peculiar scent that brings back a world. In the other hand, I cup the treasured memory of two years that we passed on American soil, when, for two Christmases running, we put nothing but ornaments of birds in a Virginia-grown balsam. Those Christmases are lit for me. My lanky body brimmed with contentment, partially due to the sight of the beautiful ceramic, straw and tinsel birds among the green bows, but mostly at the thrill of sameness. There is something in the spirit of a child that rises and takes wing in response to ritual.

I have been trying to institute rituals in my life ever since I was born. "We will eat goose on Christmas Eve every year," I declare, "And take a walk after dinner." I make the assembled company vow to cleave to this pattern with me. But each year, no matter how hard I try--it is as if the patterns of my childhood cannot be defied--the Christmas meal is utterly different. One year, planning a Christmas gathering with friends who spent their most romantic summer on Crete, we, in great excitement, decide to cook a Greek feast on Christmas eve. We celebrate the winter festival by gorging on garlic lamb, spanakopita, rice with cinnamon and cloves, four kinds of olives, and retsina. Another year, dreaming of Vermont from a South American country, I collect all the ingredients for roast beef and yorkshire pudding.

As for hallowed partakings of food and drink, my parents brought forward no eating or drinking habits from their families save one: my father's mother sent one of her children out every morning to bring home glazed donuts for breakfast. To this day, following in his mother's footsteps, one of my father's chief pleasures is to head out in the wan morning light to search for pastries. My Hoosier mother, raised on roast beef and home-grown potatoes grown on the farmstead, is an international gourmet. She turns out a superb rijs taffel as easily as a fragrant, steaming Chinese hot pot. The closest I have come to experiencing the reverence Hampl felt on watching the opening of the dandelion wine occurred for me in Patagonia. There, I savored the sight of my aged friend Don Pepe imbibing, from a wine-skin, a stream of thin red wine as we sampled together the first lamb of the season.

Perhaps children are never satisfied, for, in spite of the glamour of my many-countried childhood, there is something in me that yearns for pea-soup rootedness. It is an atavistic longing. A yearning for thick soled shoes, for a deep-sunk barn, for a muddy pasture to which my family--a family extending beyond the nuclear knot--lays claim.

And these yearnings of mine run beyond ubiquitous, idle leanings toward the greener pasture, or the road not taken. This river of yearning has sundry branches riding in its flow. One of the stouter branches: When I arrived in the United States for a two year stay, at age seven, I (blond and green-eyed) was taunted by my classmates, who had been informed about my birth place, for being a Jap. In one momentary flash at Radnor Elementary in Bethesda, Maryland, I came into a double awareness: first, that I did not belong in my own country, and second, that others did belong; that others had geographical locations, points on the map, streets lined with wide-branching trees, where they felt "at home."

The reading of memoirs by people who spent entire unbroken childhoods in places such as the Bronx or St. Paul rouses in me a hunger for the home-made dumplings my own childhood did not serve up. Strong emotion stirs and steams in my heart.

This is the crux of it: I have a deep and absorbent longing for an ethnic girlhood. In the soft, pulsing center of my heart, I long for a Catholic girlhood, or for a Jewish one. Often I have wondered, during childhood and adulthood and in all seriousness, whether I am actually Irish way back, or Jewish, or whether there is secretive French blood trickling in my veins. If I could just find out, it might solve everything.

There you have it. The confession from the Embassy princess. The fundamental truth is this: I long for my St. Paul friend Claudia's grandmother's rainbow jello salad.

While I don't feel legitimately American--as American as St. Paul's Patricia Hampl or Bronxian Kate Simon--much of my quandary could be seen as all-American. My dilemma could be simply that of the child of self-made Americans of humble past, the quandary of the child of poor natives as opposed to that of the first generation immigrants' child.

My parents, both from relatively lean beginnings, left behind their midwestern families when they were in their mid-twenties to seek their fortunes in the great world. My mother, the ninth child of a strong, proud, Quaker forester, turned her back to the log house and truck garden in Henryville, Indiana, and forged a new self as a foreign service officer's wife, a teacher, a physical therapist, and the ministrant to the crippled children of several Asian countries. My father, likewise, left behind his family's crumpled yellow house in St. Louis, he joined the C.I.A., and he never glanced back.

To my girlhood question, "What are we?" my parents, a little curious that I should ask, replied, "Oh, I don't know, Sweetie. We're mongrels, I guess. Probably some mix of English and German." My mother sometimes added, "My brother thinks we're from the Channel Isles, but I don't know that he really knows." My parents had little interest in their families' origins. They were headed for the horizon.

At times it is essential for a young person who desires to put flesh on his dreams to leave home, for good and finally. In order to escape limitation, or to <u>create</u> a life rather than slip into a given one, he or she must roar off and leave home in the dust. My parents were cooked in a mold different from that of recent immigrants, but just as American. Their skeletons are constructed of the bones of the Americans of the frontier--those who depart known turf, forge into the wilderness alone and prosper through grit and determination.

Meanwhile, brought up far from want, I poke in the dust for the past my parents left behind.

The summer that I was eleven my family took home leave from my father's post in the rainy cobblestone city of The Hague, and travelled to the home of my mother's sister in Indiana. There, in New Albany, a tiny town set on the grimy flats near Louisville, I, the little girl raised on the scarlet, clanging funeral processions of Taiwan, the subtle silences of the Japanese, and the gorgeous cream puffs of Europe, was wakened to a life dream that would dog me forever after.

It was a glorious summer. Hot and sweaty and perfect. Every day, my cousins and I grabbed our suits, ambled down wide streets lined with small bungalows, cut through back yards and alleys, and ended up at the neighborhood swimming pool. There, luxuriously parentless, we cannon-balled and dolphined all day, watched over by a life guard who was my cousins' neighbor, and ordering hamburgers and cokes whenever we happened to be hungry. Every now and then a neighbor child would dash in, breathless, to deliver a message from my mother and Aunt Norma, giving us instructions as to when to come home, or where to meet them for an ice cream outing to Ben Franklin's. Usually we played in the cool, light-lanced turquoise of the pool until after five, returning home just as the platters of fried chicken and potato salad were being placed on the long picnic table in the backyard. At the pool, my cousins, and my mother's family, were known by everyone, and I was immediately accepted as one of the Guernsey clan. The sense of being known, of not having to explain who I was--Randy would simply say "This is my cousin," and that took care of it--was sweetest pleasure. As the foreign child of a "diplomat," I was used to having to offer polite explanations for myself, so this sense of being one of a gang was vanilla ice cream to me.

My brother and I slept on the top floor with the three cousins, in the carpeted, low-ceilinged attic where the air conditioning was a little too cold. Contented as a cocooned caterpillar in my sleeping bag, I read late into the darkness, after the nightly pillow fight, squirming a bit under my sunburn.

I enjoyed every second I passed in New Albany. I loved having an uncle--known to everyone in town by first name--who owned a car repair garage. I loved the old ladies with names like Thelma or Violet, who seemed always to be on their porches tending pots of flowers, and who waved as we played kick the can in the street after dinner. I loved the humble bungalows all the same but different, the nightly smells of barbecues, and the back yards with round, standing pools. It was a thrill to be able to dash headlong through the streets. More than anything, I loved having relatives. I fancied that I looked like my cousin Randy who was born only a week or two after me. Secretly I imagined he might even be my twin.

These New Albany days became my image of quintessential America. It was a vision of a bountiful, rooted, family-stuffed, unattainable life that I craved badly, like M-n-M's and Ripleys chips, throughout my exotic, itinerant childhood. From country to country, I took a picture of the New Albany summer with me in my carry-on bag.

Though half of me throve on my family's ramblings from place to place, the other half of me always yearned for a life in middle America.

In 1987, on departing graduate school, I struck out for the middle of America, to Minnesota, to try to take possession of America, of regionality, of home. I had decided to try for the dream.

On my arrival in St. Paul, all signs were auspicious. We found a white frame house with a front porch that exactly fitted my image of a house on main street. We moved in and spread out, delighting in the light, oak-trimmed rooms. Our neighbors--the kind on whom you can drop in for coffee any time and who bring over tuna hot dish when your babysitter has quit and your husband is out of town--quickly became fast friends. Our daily life assumed an easy, reliable pace. My drive to the university took only fifteen minutes, along gracious elm-lined Summit Avenue and Mississippi River Boulevard, and my husband arrived home before five thirty every day, at the end of a twenty minute drive on a nearly vacant highway. Our preschool age daughter was looked after by a native of St. Paul who not only taught her to bake Irish soda bread, but to dance an Irish jig. It was a city that put family first; to our great pleasure after the pressures of Cambridge, over-work was the exception rather than the rule. Within the year of our arrival, U.S. News and World Report validated my wisdom by designating my chosen city the most livable one in the country.

St. Paul lived up to my initial impression and to its magazine reputation. It is a lovely town, composed of blocks of well-kept houses laid out on a grid. A person of almost any income can afford a house and picket fence, and the neighborhood I lived in was an interesting mix of older people who had grown up in the houses they lived in, young politicos, plumbers, and high tech consultants. The St. Paul bookstores, jammed with avid, critical, down-jacketed readers, are wonderful--overflowing with all the latest books. Theatre, better funded in Minnesota than in most states, is both polished and bold. There are festivals for the book and for the tree, and a hardy social conscience resides in the bones of every Minnesotan.

At first it seemed as though Minnesota was the place for me. But, as slowly and surely as the snow piling up against the house, my restlessness grew. And, in the end, the dream didn't work.

"Why?," I asked myself over and over month after month. "Why, after nearly four years, can't I, the ace adapter, adapt to St. Paul?"

I could provide all sorts of reasons for my inability to cozy into the logical spot for cozying--reasons ranging from the most simple-minded to those slightly more profound. I could explain that, in such a family-oriented place, having no extended family nearby was a handicap and I felt out of the stream. Or I could say that I simply couldn't get the hang of Minnesota-speak. As a diplomat's child, I was accustomed to rather formal conversation in which the two conversants alternated asking questions, to show interest in each other's lives and thoughts. The questions I asked in St. Paul didn't elicit the responses I expected. Over and over again, I sensed that with my questions I was being too intense, or nosy, and my attempts at conversation often resulted in monosyllabic replies or withdrawal by many of the shy, reserved breed of Minnesotans. What is more, I was unable to converse about the appropriate topics; the duck season, for instance, or the Dayton's daisy sale. Those subjects weren't in my repertoire.

I could tell you that the wordlessness and emotional mildness of the people drove me to drink. Or that I just couldn't adjust to the pallor, the blond curls, and that I missed darker skin with a desperation. Or that there was nowhere to go on weekends--no New England towns to explore, or seascapes to comb; that I felt closed into the middle of the continent. Or I could earnestly explain that you have to grow up there to fit in. But really, the hitch was in me. I had failed at becoming regional. I could not find an easy chair in that America.

By my last year in Minnesota my body started mulching up with winter dread in mid-July, just a month-and-a-half after the sun had melted the previous year's snow. But more than the sub-zero weather, it was the pain at not fitting in that ached.

Traveling to Minnesota to take my new job, I was sure I could find a home there. After all, I was in my own country, and I was going deep into its heart. It turned out that my assumptions were not sturdy. As much as in Japan or Borneo, I felt myself to be a foreigner in Minnesota. And the discomfort was even more acute there because I was feeling out of place in a place where I "ought" to feel at home. The assumption, on the part of myself and the Minnesotans, that I was, at core, the same as they, bogged me down and tripped me up. I looked the same, but the Minnesota clothes just didn't fit.

Someone's grandmother in a calico dress and starched apron, tending her pink roses. That is what brought a lump to my throat as I walked through St. Paul the last days before I left for the East. I wept as I walked beside the delphinium-laced and morning glory-spangled houses, but I had to face it. I had to square with who I was.

These are the facts, the legacy of my journeying childhood: I have to live in or near a big city, on the continental crust of the country, where there are residents of many hues. I was immediately soothed, I recall, when I arrived in Seattle for a year's stay in 1977 and was surrounded by Asian-American faces. They were the eyes and noses of my first seven years. Aside from an ethnic brew, I need a sea nearby. For its shorelessness, and for its sense of possibility. As much as anything, I need to either live among foreigners, or be one myself. It is a burden to live in a place where I am, by virtue of my nationality, supposed to fit in. I need to live in a place where I can hear foreign languages in the grocery store, and where I can spend time steeped in foreign cultures as idiosyncratic and tradition-sodden as those of the St. Paulites, but without having to try to belong. To feel alive, I need to be able to listen to the words of foreigners, to sense the emotional cadences behind their syllables, and try to understand the unique ways in which they vision life. My upbringing has made of me an ethnographer to the marrow.

With the sight of Dutch rainscapes and Bornean junglelands among which I drifted during my youth, I drank in a set of attitudes. These perspectives make up the contents of my traveling trunk; they are the inheritance from my particular childhood. First, I have a penchant for putting myself in new situations. While this places me in the position of having to struggle to survive, both emotionally and logistically, over and over again, there is an intoxication that accompanies a landing on unfamiliar streets. With my past well behind me, far across continents or seas, I can be anything. I can cast off an uncomfortable self. I have a fresh chance. I can--at least in theory, and theory is heady stuff--by a simple decision of will, become a brazen sexy clown, or a tailored literary dame.

A second legacy of my upbringing is that I am, by inmost nature, a chameleon, a sponge, a being of multiple selves. When I arrive anywhere I observe the mores and values of the place and then seek to mimic them, becoming, in a sense, each time, someone new.

It is common to human nature that when one doesn't have the standard childhood, or the standard anything, cognitive dissonance takes the upper hand, and what one does have becomes the grand thing. A third allotment from my childhood rises from this human tendency. Since living in one place for an extended period was not a possibility during my youth, departure, rather than remaining, has, for me, a silvery glow. I know very well how to leave, but possess almost no knowledge, in my storehouse, of how to stay somewhere. And staying somewhere for very long, such as over four years, has appeared to me dull and uninviting. For a couple of years I was comfortable clad as a Minnesotan, but, inexorably and inevitably, I started to miss my previous selves, restlessness set in, and I needed to move along.

A fourth item that lies among the yellowing Belgian lace in my trunk is a hefty dose of ambivalence. As a result of having seen many diametrically opposed, and equally successful, ways of conducting most kinds of affairs, I am laden with an irrepressible habit of seeing two sides to everything. I, unlike women raised within deep-dredged traditions, cannot state with conviction, "This is the way to make pot roast." I almost always carry within me at least two simultaneous and not always compatible recipes.

A gut sense that I do not have a rightful place in any setting, that I do not quite fit in, and that I have no right to shape what goes on, not being a proper member, is a fifth bestowal of my upbringing. I will ever have this shade of vulnerability. I will always live along in discomfort, certain that, in order to fit into a group or place in which I have set myself down, I must change something deep and vague and essential in myself. This perspective, an accurate one if one has the intent of trying to slip into another culture, affords one the sense of always walking on eggs, of feeling like a mouse scuttling around a table of feasters. And, always, of standing outside, looking in. The awareness that others do belong at the table has supplied me regular stabs of sharp pain.

It is the longing for America, of course, that takes up the largest space in the trunk of my traveling childhood. Like a bulky winter coat jammed on top, it cloaks the other items in the trunk. Yearning for ritual and community and belonging is the horse I ride.

I have lost something sweet and irreplaceable.

But another thing is equally true. I have sauntered away with riches.

I carry suitcases of sky-land images and musical notes and fragrances from all over the world--delicious delicacies on which I may feast at any time. I have fingered the batiks and smelt the incense of Bornean bazaars and so, know to seek them out again. I am eager for the new. Like my parents and the American pioneers, I am ready to ride off into the sunset for a look over the next hill. I breathe a pure and rarified air when I engage in conversation with foreigners--a kind of oxygen I would trade for nothing. I love a dozen different houses in six or seven countries. My childhood has given me the gift of memory, of observation, of the need to describe what I see. Out of one kind of loss I have fashioned a life work--work devoted to ferreting out the beliefs of others, of digging in the earth for others' roots. I am well acquainted with the thorough pleasure of living vicariously.

I hold a sense of place very different from that of the writers of the deep-rooted ethnic memoirs into which I have been dipping. A sense of place no less treasured or weighty. Place, for me, is a marker of change, chance, of opportunity. Just as for the child raised in one spot, each of the places in which I have lived or visited is cherished, potent. The castle in Friesland with the fabulous breakfast. The lobster meal on the beach in Nha Trang. These various meals, these culinary memories, are my tradition--and perhaps kept more tenderly for their fleeting nature. Now that I am no longer there, I treasure Minnesota as one of my past beloved places. Already, the breakfasts at the No Wake Cafe, a barge docked along the Mississippi in St. Paul, assume their place in my mental carton of memorable meals.

My body floods with an odd but blissful sort of comfort in a strange hotel, with a culture to decipher spread out, like a grand meal, on the street below the window. And once down on the street itself I have simultaneous responses: I am both fascinated and homesick.

Will I ever feel like a legitimate American? I don't know. I am most comfortable and most myself as a foreigner. I might be most at home living part-time in the United States and the other part in another country. Or perhaps at a spot mid-way across a sea. I'm not sure.

One of these days, perhaps I will move to New England, to give the ethnic girlhood another shot. Or maybe I will move to Nepal. In the meanwhile, I am going along fairly happily, living in Washington and missing the buffalo plaids and blond heads of St. Paul.

There are two sure things. I will always be filled with longing, and I will continue on with my one habit. Every weekend I will travel out in the dove-grey of early morning in search of pastries.

Sara Taber is a writer, independent scholar, and human development specialist. She grew up in an internationally mobile family.

GREAT ADVANTAGES

by Rachel Miller Schaetti

Despite the drawbacks of family separation and the very real adjustment on the permanent return to the States, a child growing up abroad has great advantages. He learns, through no conscious act of learning, that thoughts can be transmitted in many languages, that skin color is unimportant, that non-Christians can be deeply and devotedly religious. He takes it for granted that some cities have skyscrapers and others have houseboats, that certain things are sacred or taboo to some people while to others they're meaningless, that the ordinary word of one area is a swearword in another.

We have lived in Tulsa for 5 years, longer than I have ever lived consecutively in one place before. So I am having my first real chance to watch American children growing up in an American community. I am struck again and again by the fact that so much of the sociology, feeling for history, geography, questions on other religions, etc., that our friends' children try to understand through textbooks, my sisters and I acquired just by living.

Rachel Schaetti wrote "Great Advantages" in April 1957 at the age of 33. A U.S. American global nomad (now deceased), Ms. Schaetti was married to a Swiss global nomad and raised three children in ten countries on four continents. These are Ms. Schaetti's final comments on a questionnaire from Jack O. Claypoole, George Williams College.

WHY WE WORRY ABOUT RAISING KIDS OVERSEAS

by Nancy Piet-Pelon

[Reprinted with permission from the April 1988 issue of
The Foreign Service Journal.]

It often appears to parents living overseas that all children living in the United States play first-chair clarinet, star on all-star soccer teams, and win prizes in science fairs, poetry contests, and debate meets. Feelings of inadequacy, bordering on guilt, do not come because so many other children show talent, but from the fact that our equally talented children are overseas with us and thus can participate in few of these activities.

Not the least of our worries is that they may have to compete with these accomplished paragons someday. Will they be able to? Many small posts have too few children to organize a soccer team, and the school may not own a clarinet or even an orchestra chair. Rather than joining school activities, our children's accomplishments may consist of simply adjusting to yet another new set of friends. Even larger posts may have important obstacles to learning and development.

Of course, they may also have the chance for adventures of which dreams are made. Our son, for instance, walked for five days on a school trek in sight of the breathtaking Himalayas. He got neither blisters nor dysentery and returned home with a sense of having done something great.

But it is time to ask again, Is what our kids experience overseas enough? Does it prepare them, even in a clearly different way, for being adults in the competitive society of America? Or does the Foreign Service lifestyle condemn them to never being at home in the country that is supposed to be their home? Will there be positive results from all of the moving and adjusting and the stress that it creates? In short, will we one day wake up and find that our children are the victims, rather than the beneficiaries, of our ambitions?

These hard questions are rarely asked in the large cities, with many activities available in the international schools. In small posts, however, these concerns become paramount. I am one who considered life overseas far more enriching than anything I had seen in the United States until we arrived in Kathmandu, a small place with a small school. Since the majority of Foreign Service families do find themselves in the small places of the world at one time or another, these concerns are important.

In wrestling with these problems, several considerations are important depending on the size of the post and the school: opportunities to develop academic, artistic, or athletic skills; enhancements parents are willing to provide; flexibility of the entire family; and expectations for the future.

When a school or community is small, there are clear disadvantages. A class of 12 children may have an advantage in unity and "family feeling," but on the days when one child is "odd man out," he or she will experience enormous pain because there is no maneuvering room. There are no other groups to move into, no other friends to select from. Especially for teenagers, who need to sort out their values and make decisions for their own lifestyle, a small environment can be deadly.

Academically, however, small schools can be very effective. The family atmosphere, particularly in the lower grades, can give security to the child. The teachers know every student and can be very caring. However, on the negative side, a child is easily typed. If he or she is going through a rebellious period, a child can find it more difficult to break out of that pattern in a small environment. Course work in a small school is limited. Very often special teachers are not available. Equipment is not the latest and, if the school depends on local-hire teachers, their changing circumstances can mean disruptions in mid-year.

Large schools, on the other hand, tend to offer the same academic and athletic programs as schools in the United States: Academic programs are often enhanced by the International Baccalaureate curriculum, which allows students to extend themselves academically. Socially there is more choice, both in terms of selecting friends and activities. In large settings, the overseas school may have many advantages...

There is more in the overseas environment than the school, although that will always be a primary influence. A small post can be good for children and provide a safe locale for family activities. However, teens need more than family. They need places where they can congregate and have their own activities, they need to have the experience and responsibilities of employment, the chance to develop skills, and the challenges of academic and athletic competition. Teens can be very bored and discontented in environments that do not challenge them. They yearn for and need the opportunity to do what they need to do to grow up...

What about the opportunities to develop skills -- academic, artistic, or athletic? The overseas environment, whether large or small, has some advantages in this area. Language teachers are often native speakers. Children do not only read about the wonders of the world, they visit them -- the pyramids, 9th century Hindu and Buddhist shrines, Macchu Pichu. The opportunity to see the wonders of the world can stretch their intellect and bring lessons to life. Artistic skill can be developed in unique ways. It is possible to learn Balinese dance and gamelon music in Jakarta, to play the sitar in New Delhi, and to practice Chinese brush painting and calligraphy and take batik lessons in many Asian posts. While ordinary piano lessons may be hard to get, many replacements for artistic expression are possible. Athletic opportunities are different as well. There are more chances for inexpensive lessons in individual sports. On the other hand, team sports competition is often not possible, at least on a regular basis. Many posts have to be content with occasional competition and relatively little first-class coaching.

Parents play an important role in the satisfaction children get living overseas. Their attitude is all important. If they are positive and excited about living at a post, the children will be too. And when opportunities for growth are not available, parents can create or provide some of them in different ways. Some parents sacrifice vacation plans so that the children can go home each summer. When children are young, vacation activities can include community recreation programs, camps, or extra classes. For teens the sojourn home can mean the opportunity to obtain a driver's license -- an important badge signifying a rite of passage -- or to work at a fast-food establishment, a real cultural leveler. It may not sound very exciting to the parents involved, but it certainly eases the child's adjustment later.

Flexibility is another factor. If a family arrives at a post and finds the school inadequate, or the setting not right for the child, then they should look at alternatives. The American family, unlike the British, finds the boarding school alternative unpalatable, but practically speaking a boarding school offers a life which caters to the young. And any other alternative, such as cutting the tour short, involves weightier decisions.

When discussing alternatives, any family has to ask whether the child is getting enough to grow on at different stages in the overseas setting. My feeling is that most children are very enriched overseas until about the age of 10 or 11. In those early years, a concerned teacher, a small circle of friends, and caring and aware parents can provide all the emotional, physical, and intellectual stimulation the child requires. The opportunities of travel and participating in a new culture are all added in the positive column. But after those years, I am not sure that the small overseas setting does offer enough, and the larger posts need to be judged on an individual basis.

Finally, the expectations for the child, his or her own and the family's, must be taken into consideration. My comments have been written from the point of view that the eventual goal for the child of a Foreign Service family is to return and fit into the American environment. This is the reason for concern and for helping kids stay abreast of that culture. They need to be able to develop the skills that will help them succeed. But, perhaps those are not the expectations of the family. Rather, since the child is being raised overseas, the expectations are different. They do not expect their children to go to university in the States or even live there, they do not expect them to be successful Americans, but rather to be successful international citizens.

For me, the problem with that is we risk raising children who rather than being at home everywhere, are at home nowhere. They have not been given the opportunity to learn the skills required for survival in American culture, yet they have not been socialized to fit into any other one culture either. It seems that we have to acculturate our children to fit in somewhere, even though at some point they might say they plan to live in Paris or Timbuktu, not Falls Church or Bethesda. Our duty is to help them have the skills to make these choices.

Bringing our children overseas is not harmful in itself, but we must reevaluate it regularly. In the lives of each of our children there may be times when living with us overseas is not the best, either because of the post itself or because the child is simply at a point where he or she needs more than that post offers. It is the role and responsibility of the parents, and children as they get older, to evaluate the experience and make the most appropriate decision for the moment.

Nancy Piet-Pelon, a family-planning consultant, writer on cross-cultural issues, and wife of an AID Foreign Service officer, currently lives in Bangladesh with her husband and son.

NOSTALGIA

by Ursula Lindsey

I arrived from Rome the 20th of June. Everything here is still utterly unknown, so totally different for me: our house and our car and our neighborhood, the streetlights and the food and the stores.

I'm carrying eight years of friendships and experiences and sights, of small, unnoticed knowledge and love for small, "unthought-of" things that have no link to or acknowledgement in this new place.

Physically, I am here. But everything that belongs to me, everything that defines me, is on the other side of the Atlantic Ocean, in the old, sunny streets where my Italian friends laugh and yell, in impossibly far away Rome . . . .

Rome may not be any hotter than Washington, but it looks it. It seems warm and cluttered and dusty, like a drawer full of old woollen socks bathed in late afternoon sun. Washington, however, seems cool and clean, with its dark green trees and neat brick houses, with its wide, white monuments and enormous museums. There's a different light in these two cities: Rome glows from the mellow-colored buildings and breaks through in lazy golden shafts, among the crowds and crooked streets.

I don't know Washington, D.C. and I find that even as I begin to discover it, I realize how much there is yet to learn. I am pained at my vague, bitter nostalgia for all that I knew. I am finding it easier to like Washington; it's a big, beautiful, open city. I know that here, in the near future, I can be happy, as long as I learn to cope with change and believe in time.

Ursula Lindsey was 15 years old when she wrote "Nostalgia." She and her family have lived in China and Italy and will depart for Ankara, Turkey in the summer of 1994.

WORLD-WISE KIDS
Special Qualities Mark These Global Nomads

by Nina Killham

[Reprinted with permission from the February 17, 1990 issue of
The Washington Post.]

He's blond-haired, blue-eyed, and Timothy Mechem still thinks of
himself as East African. He was born 21 years ago to American
missionary parents in Zambia and never stepped off the continent until
1985. He speaks Chichewa, understands Swahili and, to this day, his
accent is as thick as honey.

Mechem is a Global Nomad -- someone having spent his formative
years living outside his passport country -- U.S. or otherwise -- with
parents sponsored by various institutions, namely the Foreign Service,
government or international agencies, the military, church missions,
international corporations or business.

On the average, a Global Nomad has lived in six different countries by
the time he is 18 years old -- his cultural identity becoming gradually
unglued from that of his monocultural parents and forming into a new
sensibility. Global Nomads include the Kennedy children, George
Bush's children, John Denver and Brook Astor.

Though no one counted all the Global Nomads living in the
Washington area, it's probably safe to say that with sponsors like the
Pentagon, State Department and World Bank, this city must have the
highest percentage in the country. In 1988, the number of Americans
living abroad reached 2,054,148, with an estimated 230,000 of them
American students attending overseas schools. About 10,000 students
graduate from such schools each year.

A silent minority, Global Nomads now are being touted across the
country by such groups as Global Nomads International, Mu Kappa
(especially for missionary youths) and Interaction, Inc. (for the care of
youth and families in the expatriate community) as possessing unique
characteristics -- distinct from those who grew up in their native
culture.

These include superior diplomacy, flexibility, linguistic ability, patience and sophistication. On the down side, there's insecurity in relationships, unresolved grief stemming from constantly leaving friends throughout childhood, and rootlessness.

One of the most difficult questions Global Nomads can be asked is where they are from. The common response will be, "when?" Says David Pollock, director of Interaction, Inc., "I know a girl who said 'I'm from Egypt.' I asked, 'How long did you live in Egypt?' and she answered, 'Well, I actually never lived in Egypt. The last time I lived at home we lived in Mozambique, but my parents are in Egypt.'" Home becomes not a geographic notion, but an emotional one.

Anna Maripuu, the daughter of a Swedish United Nations official, who has just finished her masters degree in international affairs and economics at George Washington University, was born in Sweden, lived in the United States from ages 6 to 12 and then lived in developing countries before returning to the United States for her college studies.

It's a life, she says, that produces misunderstandings -- "I'll mention home in a conversation three times and it can mean three different places." In her mind, the differences are clear, she says, but her friends do not understand how her loyalties can be so neatly split.

And often after several years abroad, American Global Nomads return to find the "home" in the United States is yet another unknown culture to learn. This is the time, says Norma McCaig, founder of Global Nomads International in Washington, when the flexibility, patience and diplomacy they have acquired through the years need to be at full tilt.

Stephanie Turco, 24, the daughter of a Foreign Service officer, and who lived in India, Pakistan and Afghanistan from the time she was 2, came back to the States with a gold ring in her nose. "People thought I didn't speak English. They would talk about me in the elevator. 'What's that thing in her nose, how ugly.' I didn't say anything. I was so embarrassed, but it made me feel very alienated for a long time. I didn't trust people for a long time."

For these dependents, assimilation does not necessarily end their odyssey. Many Global Nomads speak of an internal clock that continues to ring every few years, prodding them to pack up and move. Some call it itchy feet, some call it ants-in-the-pants. "I call it having sand in their shoe," says Ruth Hill Useem, professor emeritus of sociology, education and anthropology at Michigan State University, who coined the phrase Third Culture Kid (TCK).

According to Useem, the average TCK changes colleges twice. This rootlessness not only has a strong negative effect on careers, it sabotages relationships, too. Marriages between TCKs and others often are strained by the TCK's perpetual craving for a change of scene.

Jim Bradford, an independent radio producer who recognizes the destructive pattern in his love life, says: "I am not staying long enough to see a relationship through." Bradford followed his father to Japan, Paraguay, Peru and Honduras until his 18th birthday and then continued his nomadic life on his own by working in Ecuador, the Dominican Republic, Guatemala and Nicaragua. His internal clock, he says, rings loud and clear. "I feel the urge every two or three years. In fact, I'm trying to go back to Latin America right now."

And even if they do settle down, there is a tendency to remain unattached. It's not uncommon to run into a Global Nomad who has lived in the same apartment for more than 10 years, but still has a portable TV, unbreakable dishes, folding furniture and unpacked boxes in the basement.

Anthony Bates, also the dependent of a Foreign Service officer, who lived in London, Paris, Hong Kong and Berlin by the time he was 12, says he tends to feel unattached emotionally. "There are times when I don't want to but I am; I can't help it. Other times it's useful." Like the other day when a fight broke out in front of him at the line to buy Metro fare cards and he stood back and watched as if it were a movie. "In some ways I'm always the foreigner, separate and apart, but in some ways I'm always at home. It's strange. The two things can coexist."

Most characteristics of a multicultural upbringing, however, are positive and are the focus of groups like TCK Student Services, Tim Mechem's fledgling support group for TCKs at American University. "The TCKs don't realize that they are special," says Mechem. "I want to tell them it's okay that they're weird."

Mechem remembers feeling weird himself when he realized his Sub-Saharan African mentality set him apart from other American students. "We tend to talk slower, we tend to take things in and think about them before responding. We like to take one task at a time and finish, rather than doing a million things at once. And we tend to be very fatalistic. What happens, happens."

Mechem says he feels comfortable with the atmosphere at American University, where it is not unusual to walk into a common area, he says, "and run into a Chinese girl and a Mali student cracking jokes with a Swiss, all in Russian."

Some Global Nomads find that even their English needs translation. Says Anthony Bates, "I'll say I'm mad about my flat and Americans will think I'm angry about my flat tire, when I'm really saying I love my apartment."

According to Ruth Useem, 90 percent of TCKs are conversant in at least one other language. Also, Global Nomads, through studies, have shown to be good observers, less judgmental and less prejudicial.

"I feel that I can easily deal with different personalities, different nationalities," says Stephanie Turco. "I'm used to juggling. I sort of slide into uptight or different situations. I'm not made nervous by wondering whether or not I'm doing the right thing."

Most important, says Interaction, Inc.'s David Pollock, a Global Nomad tends to have a three-dimensional view of the world. "A TCK will read a headline in a newspaper, and can often smell the smells, hear the sounds, and identify with the pain and disaster a half a world away," says Pollock. "Their world view is the expanded world view."

Jim McCaffrey, vice president of Training Resources Group, a management and developmental consulting firm in Alexandria, has a different perception. Global Nomads, he says, have not necessarily cornered the market on intercultural skills. "I don't make the *a priori* assumption that a Global Nomad is a better multiculturalist. I've seen people who lived all over the world who've been as insensitive as a brick."

In McCaffrey's opinion, the ideal candidate for an intercultural job is a Global Nomad with the double experience of living in a foreign country as a child and again as an adult. "I want someone who has lived there and made something out of it, who has thought about it -- one doesn't necessarily lead to the other."

Says Pollock: "We have to recognize that part of the role of the third-cultured people of today is to be the culture bridge and culture brokers for the whole generation." The Global Nomad of today, he says, is the prototype of the citizen of the 21st century.

Nina Killham served with her Foreign Service family in Copenhagen and Brussels during her childhood. She earned her Bachelors degree in Political Science from William & Mary and went to work as a staff writer for the Washington Post. She currently writes movie scripts in Venice, California.

CULTURAL EDUCATIONAL EXPERIENCES

by Anders Lundahl

In my lifetime, I have entered new schools about once every four years moving from the States to countries overseas. Besides having personal experience in this subject, I have also seen how it is for other kids to come to a new school. I have had the chance to observe what feelings they have and could compare them to my own. There are certain problems that you encounter when moving away from what you call home and entering a new world where you must adjust to the way people act. The biggest problem is having to part with old friends and then making new ones.

When you are first told that you will be moving away sometime in the future, you start thinking about what it will be like in this new place and of course what the people there will be like. No matter how much time you are given in advance to help you adjust to the fact that you are leaving, it is never enough. You try to spend more time with your friends and try to enjoy the rest of the time together, but your thoughts are always hindered by the idea of moving. Having dealt with these feelings personally, I can safely say that you do not realize what good friends you have until you are hundreds of miles from home. Often you start to be more cynical of what your friends do as sort of a natural instinct so that maybe you will not miss them so much. But in the end it only hurts you because when you are gone you start to think that maybe you wasted those last months or weeks that you had with them. That is only the first part of your social problems when you move from place to place; making new friends most often is just as hard as leaving old ones.

Your first day of school is always the worst and there is good reason for it to be. If you have never lived in the area before and know absolutely nobody, then there is no one to talk to and you keep all your feelings inside. All you think about the first couple of days is how much you miss your old friends, how much you hate your new school, and how much you hate your parents for doing this to you. If you have lived in the area before and still know people, then the adjustment is much easier since your old friends will introduce you to new people. But if you have never lived there before, then it is solely up to you and the way you act determines the kind of friends you meet. If you are a very distinct person, then it does not really take long to find the group of people that you will get along with. If you play sports, you can meet people through that; if you are interested in music, maybe you could join the band; if you smoke, you could meet people before or after school where everyone goes to smoke. How hard you must try to find new friends is directly related to your personality and whether or not you want a lot of friends or are happy with just a few. Oftentimes new people try to act differently than they really are in order to fit in. This will only hurt you in the long run because people will start to see you are a fake and not want to be your friend. Even though leaving and making new friends is the hardest part about moving to a new school, there are other problems that arise, such as trying to adjust to the new school's curriculum and rules.

Often when you move to a new school there is a change in what is required of you and in what you need to graduate. This often upsets people because maybe you did things in your old school that are not needed. That makes you feel as if it was a waste of time, which just adds to the emotions that you are feeling. It also works the other way in that you may be ahead of everyone in your new school, which means you need to do less work which oftentimes helps you in adjusting. Then there are the rules, which differ from school to school, such as being able to leave campus for lunch which you might have been able to do at your last school but which you might not be able to do at your new school. Whether it goes for you or against you, it can build up or ease the emotions that are swirling in your head. The most important thing that you must keep in mind is that it is not that important and that you cannot let it bring you down. You have to deal with it and try not to let it show because people around you might think less of you if you always look upset.

Another problem that you might come across is life at home. Chances are that your parents are having a hard time making friends as well. Often kids do not take this into consideration, thinking that their parents moved away from their old home just to hurt them. This is not true at all and it takes a while for kids to realize this. Whatever the reason for the move, you should not take your emotions out on your mom or dad.

No matter how bad you think things are, you must always believe that there are better times ahead, because there are and you will eventually find a place to fit in. All you really have to do is keep a good attitude and everything will turn out all right.

Anders Lundahl lived in Muscat, Oman; New Delhi, India; Maputo, Mozambique; and Lusaka, Zambia during his childhood. He returned to the U.S. in Grade 11 to Langley High School and will attend George Mason University in the Fall, 1994.

HOME IS A MEMORY

by Edward Finn

Home is the doors of my old school,
a safe protection from the outside world.
Home is the cathedral ground,
wet with dew in the misty morning.
Home is where the computer examines its newest disk,
the supernintendo music flitting through the ears.
Home is where my puppy dog tries
to get her old friend to play.
Home is the view from my house in Golkoy,
the water clear as glass.
Home is where my trumpet echoes,
getting a little better every day.
Home is where my soccer shirt,
flutters like a forlorn flag.

But most important of all,
Home is but a memory,
changing while you're gone.
Home is your imagination,
caught in images, in your mind or your photo album,
something you only remember if you pull that album off a shelf
or you think a homesick thought.
Home is just a dream, gone if you go back.

Edward Finn lived in Turkey for the first five years of his life, moving to Pakistan for the next five years. After three years in Washington, D.C., Edward moved to Frankfurt. Currently, Edward is attending Groton School in Massachusetts. He was 13 years old when he wrote "Home is a Memory."

THIRD CULTURE KIDS

by Ruth Hill Useem and Richard D. Downie

[Reprinted with permission from Clyde Austin's text,
Cross-Cultural Reentry: A Book of Readings, 1986. This article
originally appeared in *Today's Education*, September-October, 1976.]

*Note: Although the following article is dated (the number of female
employees and single parents working overseas has grown since Drs.
Useem and Downie wrote this), this article is considered a "classic" in
cross-cultural literature. It offers many research findings, insights and
suggestions that are still valid today.*

The first day, the teacher stood me up in front of the class and said I
was from Singapore. The kids at that school were tough. They started
calling me Chinaman and harassing me. I didn't like being called that.
I thought it was something bad to be. I did well in school, though.
The teachers liked me, and the school was easy. The schools I went to
overseas were tougher."

"When I was 16, I came from Japan to a small town in Indiana. I
remember the first time I was out on a date -- all we did was drive
around to McDonald's and different places. The whole night! I never
really got involved much in the school life. A lot of the kids were not
planning on going to college, and so we didn't have much in common
to talk about. I think I was pretty strange for them, too."

"I think part of the problem when I came to the States was I looked
American but I did things that were not quite American. I had fun
trying to be an American. It was an act in a way."

No, these are not the observations of new immigrants or foreign
visitors. These are the reactions of American third-culture kids (TCKs)
who have come "home" after living abroad as dependents of parents
who are employed overseas. Although they have grown up *in* foreign
countries, they are not integral parts *of* those countries. When they
come to their country of citizenship (some for the first time), they do
not feel at home because they do not know the lingo or expectations of

65

others -- especially those of their own age.

Where they feel most like themselves is in that interstitial culture, the third culture, which is created, shared, and carried by persons who are relating societies, or sections thereof, to each other.

Although some Americans were living outside the United States before World War II, the great burgeoning in numbers of Americans moving overseas began after the War. Now, there are approximately 300,000 school-age American children overseas. Their fathers are missionaries; visiting professors and teachers; representatives of the U.S. government (e.g., employees of the Department of Defense, the Department of State, etc.); employees of international and multinational corporations and financial institutions (e.g., Exxon, First National City Bank, Bell Helicopter); and American employees of international organizations such as the World Health Organization and UNICEF. These fathers are usually highly educated or highly skilled people who are forging the networks that intertwine and interrelate the peoples of the world. (The mothers may be employed overseas, but in most cases, the families have moved because of the fathers' employment.)

To be sure, Americans are not the only ones involved in third cultures. For example, Japanese businessmen work and live in the United States and in Southeast Asia, and diplomats from all countries represent their governments in posts all over the world. Their dependent children can be found in university communities, in the United Nations International School in New York, in the capitals and large cities of the world, and in some of the same overseas schools as American children. In this article, we shall limit our discussion to American TCKs.

The parents' sponsor in the overseas area is crucial in determining the specific part of the third culture in which the TCKs live, the kind of school they attend, the host nationals and third country nationals they will know, and the languages they will learn. These children even have labels that reflect their parents' sponsors -- "Army brats," "MKs" (missionary kids), "biz kids," and most recently "oil kids."

Overseas, one of the first questions a TCK asks a new arrival is "What does your father do?" or "Who is your father with?" The answer helps to place young people socially. If, after returning stateside, a TCK asks such a question of a young person who has been reared here, the latter's reaction may be one of puzzlement or resentment. Unlike that of TCKs, the social life of young people reared here is not directly influenced by the father's employer.

TCKs are attached to the third culture through their parents' employers, who hold parents responsible for the behavior of their offspring. (If a dependent grossly misbehaves, he or she may be sent home, and the employer may reassign the father or terminate his employment.) Therefore, fathers take an active role in their children's lives and in making family decisions.

In one study of third culture families, only 6 of 150 TCKs reported that their mothers always or usually made final decisions about family matters. (It should be remembered that almost all overseas American families have both parents present.) Fifty-three percent of Department of Defense dependents claimed that only their fathers made final decisions, 41 percent of children of missionaries said their fathers had the final say in family decisions, and the others involved in the study, including 75 percent of children of those representing the federal government, reported that both parents and occasionally the children themselves, were involved in decision-making.

Most children and youth overseas do not resent strict parental controls, because all of them attached to the same sponsor come under similar rules and, hence, there is community reinforcement. Besides, the overwhelming majority of TCKs (close to 90 percent) like, respect, and feel emotionally attached to their parents.

There are many reasons for this. The high mobility of third-culture families, who usually move every one, two, or four years, seems to have the effect of bringing individual family members closer together. They share the common experience of moving into unfamiliar territory and offer each other mutual support in the face of change and strangeness. Parents are often the only people with whom TCKs have a continuing relationship as they move from one location to another.

American families overseas spend more time together (unless the children are in boarding school) than do their stateside counterparts -- and the time together is often not taken up with mundane aspects of living. Mothers are home managers, rather than housewives, because they usually have servants to clean up the spilled milk, make the beds, cook the meals, and chauffeur the children. As one overseas mother said, "It's amazing how pleasant conversations with children can be when you are not frantically trying to get the supper on, answer the telephone, and nag the children to pick up their clothes."

The family provides one form of continuity for TCKs. The schools offer another.

There is a remarkable similarity among the approximately 600 schools attended by American children overseas. There are also great differences.

These include variations in the size of the student body (from 10 or 12 up to 6,000 or so), differences in sponsorship (e.g., Department of Defense schools, schools assisted by the Department of State, private and entrepreneurial schools, those sponsored by corporations, and those run by Catholic orders and Protestant churches), and widely different make-ups of study bodies (e.g., from Americans only to Americans in the minority).

All of these schools place a heavy emphasis upon academic performance, and the secondary schools are college-prep oriented. The curriculum resembles that of stateside schools with the same orientation but the overseas schools usually offer enrichment courses in the local language and culture. Books and materials (which often don't arrive or come late) are generally imported from the United States.

The avowed purpose of most American-sponsored overseas schools has been to prepare American pupils for entering the mainstream of American society. Stateside schools and colleges, to the extent to which they notice TCKs at all, have been concerned with their "problems of adjustment" to their peers. Neither the overseas nor the stateside schools have seen the TCKs as people who, as adults, will be following in their parents' footsteps and fulfilling mediating roles in the increasingly conflictive but interdependent global system. Nor do the schools see that solving some "problems of adjustment" offers TCKs valuable experience that can help prepare them for their future roles -- which will probably be international.

One reason the schools lack appreciation for the great potentialities of these young people is that few educators have studied TCKs. In a bibliography on third-culture education that we compiled at the Institute for International Studies in Education, only 10 of the 50 dissertations listed concern TCKs -- how they feel and perform, what they value, what they aspire to, and how they view the world and themselves in relation to it.

(Given the rather thin reeds on which to rest generalizations about these youth and given the rapidity with which third cultures and national cultures change, we warn the readers that what we are reporting here is suggestive rather than definitive.)

One study of 150 college-enrolled TCKs of varying sponsorship and residence abroad (but all of whom had spent a minimum of one teen year overseas) produced a dramatic finding: Not one preferred to pursue a career exclusively in the United States. One-fourth named a specific place overseas where they would like to work usually the location where they had lived during their teen years); 29 percent expressed interest in following an overseas-based occupation but wanted to move from country to country; 25 percent wanted to be headquartered in the United States with periodic one- or two- year assignments abroad; and 12 percent wanted to be employed in the United States but to have opportunity for overseas job-related travel.

In order to qualify for careers in the third culture, these young people recognize that they must be well-educated and/or highly skilled. (There are few unskilled or even semiskilled third-culture occupations.) Thus they aspire, even when in secondary school, to attain college degrees, and many anticipate getting professional and advanced degrees or mastering highly specialized skills.

One important reason that TCKs want to work in an international occupation, whether pursued entirely or partially aborad, is that they feel most "at home" in third-culture networks. Only 7 percent report feeling "at home" with their peers in the United States, while 74 percent say they feel most comfortable with people who are internationally oriented and who have lived abroad.

Yet such preferences do not imply that a person is rootless or has made a "poor adjustment." As one TCK with Asian experience says, "I guess I could live anywhere and be comfortable. I have always liked to think I get along with all different people. I don't feel bothered by a lack of roots, and I don't think I have a lot of problems because of that."

To be sure, some TCKs have severe emotional problems that cannot be resolved without outside help -- and some problems not even then. But the rate is probably not greater among these foreign-experienced youth than it is among the general American population of the same age.

The reported experiences of these youth suggest that they cope rather than adjust, and, as one student of multicultural persons describes them, they become both "a part of" and "apart from" whatever situation they are in. A TCK with Asian and African experience explains, "I find myself sitting back and objectively observing Americans and American society, occasionally smiling and occasionally shaking my head. I get along comfortably with both, but then again, there is a bit of me that remains apart."

Most third-culture kids are more familiar with foreign languages than are their stateside counterparts. One researcher reports that 92 percent of the TCKs she studied learn one or more foreign languages, mostly languages used in many parts of the world, such as Spanish, German, and French. Twenty-six percent claim knowledge of languages other than, or in addition to these, such as Yoruba, Hausa, Urdu, Kijita, Swahili, Amharic, Kalagan, Marathi, Kisukuma, Chinese, and Quiche. (In U.S. public secondary schools, less than .5 percent learn languages other than French, Spanish, German, and Latin.

TCKs learn some languages in schools abroad and some in their homes or in the marketplaces of a foreign land. One-third of these youngsters are children of cross-cultural marriages and/or foreign-born parents, and they use a language other than English at home or when visiting relatives. Some pick up languages from the servants in the home or from playmates in the neighborhood.

Although most third-culture kids lose their proficiency in the foreign language when they return to an all-English-speaking environment, many pursue languages they have already learned, and some become literate in the languages they can speak. Few have emotional blockages about learning a new language -- particularly if they perceive it as useful for the career they want to pursue in the future.

What can stateside teachers do to assist these youth when they return to the United States? Perhaps the best answer is for teachers to challenge them academically, both because this gives them continuity with their past and because this helps prepare them for the futures they desire.

Teachers should also try not to make these students' uniqueness a problem for them in school. Each TCK wants to be treated as an individual, not stereotyped as the "new student from Kuwait."

One TCK who lived in the Far East sums up her feelings about her experiences upon returning to the United States in this way: "I was made to feel like an odd person, a creature from another place -- and I wasn't. I speak English, and I understand everything Americans say. My teacher and the people in the town where I was living didn't really see *me* -- they just saw the difference."

Dr. Ruth Hill Useem, Professor Emeritus of Sociology (International), Education and Anthropology at Michigan State University, is currently conducting research on Adult Third Culture Kids. Dr. Useem is renowned for her significant international research and writings on people she first dubbed "Third Culture Kids."

Dr. Richard D. Downie is Associate Director for International Studies and Programs at the University of Florida. On the Board of Directors for International Schools Services, Dr. Downie served as Director of Pupil Services at the International School, New Delhi.

SWANS, DUCKS, AND OTHER VALID CREATURES

by David C. Pollock

[Reprinted with permission from the Summer/Fall, 1992 issue of the
Global Nomad Quarterly.]

Most of us resist the stereotypes imposed upon us. However, when we
carefully consider many stereotypes, we are forced to recognize that
tendencies toward those stereotypes are present in many of us, giving
rise to conclusions that may be uncomfortable and even unfair. This is
especially true of global nomads. Global nomads are individuals with
unique combinations of characteristics born not only of cultural
variables, but also of differences in temperament, parental responses,
extent and nature of mobility, interpersonal interactions with members
of both the host and home cultures, and much more.

Although a precise profile of a global nomad can not be developed
without running the risk of stereotyping, there are some identifiable
tendencies that provide a basis for self-evaluation, self-explanation, and
self-esteem. Years of personal observation and consideration of the
research of others have led me to develop a profile of a global nomad
that, while not exhaustive, is a useful tool in thinking through the
issues associated with growing up in a multicultural milieu. Validation
for this profile has come in the form of responses like "Aha!," and
"Why didn't someone tell me this before?"

All too often, the global nomad has tried to fit into a culture that is his
or her own culture only because of a statement in a passport. Like the
ugly duckling, the global nomad has suffered the frustration of being
told to "be a duck, or at least act like a duck." This produces a variety
of results, ranging from denial of one's past to total refusal to adjust to
one's present. Parents, teachers, and even other global nomads can
contribute to extreme behaviors by insisting on conformity rather than
adjustment. By not allowing the global nomad to be a "swan," they
engender frustration and anger.

One global nomad, a diplomat from an Eastern European country,
comments that the positive side of the global nomad profile is often

denied full expression because too many global nomads become trapped in experiences associated with the negative side of the profile. Among the positive characteristics of global nomads are linguistic ability, cross-cultural skills, expanded world view (and sometimes expanded spiritual view), and advanced maturity resulting from the "stretching" experiences of the global nomad life. The expression of these characteristics is valuable in an increasingly cross-cultural and international world, a world in which the global nomad functions as a culture bridge.

A barrier to appropriate expression of the global nomad's positive characteristics is erected when the stresses of a multicultural and nomadic lifestyle are not recognized and addressed. The lack of a sense of rootedness can result in a migratory lifestyle that has a significant impact on the global nomad's academic career, life work, and family life. Mobility in itself is not the problem; it is the inner drive to be in constant motion that may be disruptive and sometimes destructive. The delicate "root system" of the global nomad's life -- based on relationships, not geography -- needs to be tended.

The many separations resulting from the nomadic lifestyle leave a residue of unresolved grief, anger, and depression. The multiple partings may also contribute to stresses in interpersonal relationships. Some global nomads decide never to allow others to get too close to them emotionally; in this way they defend themselves against the pain of separation. Many unconsciously and prematurely release themselves from relationships at the slightest hint of distancing or rejection by the other party. The lack of willingness to be vulnerable threatens intimacy even in marriage and parent-child relationships. The global nomad's independence is not altogether unhealthy, but it produces loneliness when it stands in the way of legitimate and healthy inter-reliance and trust in intimate relationships.

When they are assisted in addressing the issue of rootlessness and its effects, global nomads are able to make choices that alleviate the negative impact of their experiences. As their perspective is improved and their appreciation of their experiences expanded, they become more sensitive toward others. Understanding, prepared adults can play an important role in helping the global nomad gain this perspective.

All global nomads are not alike. They do not fit perfectly into a mold. But all global nomads need to know that it is all right to be a "swan" moving among other valuable creatures such as "ducks." By addressing the areas of stress and pain associated with their unique experiences, we can free global nomads to realize the valuable potential contained within the experience of being a multicultural person.

David Pollock is executive director of Interaction, Inc. He serves on the advisory board of the Foreign Service Youth Foundation and on the boards of directors of Mu Kappa and Global Nomads International and as Director of Intercultural Programs at Houghton College in Houghton, New York. He was also a missionary in Kenya.

CULTURAL CONFUSION ON A GLOBAL SCALE
by Leonard L. Lefkow

[Reprinted with permission from the March 6, 1994 issue of
The New York Times.]

As the big jet prepared for takeoff from New Delhi, a flight attendant
slipped into a vacant seat next to my 5-year-old daughter, who
promptly announced: "Look, Daddy, they let the servants sit down
with us on this plane."

We laugh about it now, 25 years after that embarrassing moment in
which my wife and I apologized to the flight attendant and explained -
- unsuccessfully, I'm sure -- that we had been living in India for four
years.

My wife and I consider ourselves egalitarian, but it wasn't a practice
then -- and I doubt if it is now -- for household helpers in India to sit
at the table with their employers.

It was a little early to explain the cultural realities of the Western and
Eastern worlds to a 5-year-old or, for that matter, to her 1-year-old
sister or her 7-year-old brother. They would learn during their
yearlong stay in the United States after having lived virtually all their
lives in the third world.

After all, if an innocent misunderstanding was the most serious misstep
they took, they would adapt quickly to life without household help and
the other perks of being part of a Foreign Service family abroad.

Little did we realize that we would face issues far more challenging
than a moment of embarrassment in raising youngsters who, aside
from sporadic periods in the United States, lived abroad from
childhood through most of their teen years.

After we returned from two and a half years in London, one daughter
adjusted by affecting an English accent that baffled her classmates. (It
relieved us to learn that the son of a colleague had come back
speaking English with an Italian accent.)

The other daughter, missing terribly her life in India, decided she would wear billowing pantaloons, the dress of Punjabi women, rather than the typical patched jeans and T-shirts. She didn't win any popularity contests, but we admired her individuality.

Our son, after several years in Paris, made his fashion statement with a French fisherman's shirt and a scarf draped around his neck that reached to his ankles. He spent a fairly solitary school year, but did perfect his baseball throwing arm while wrecking a garage door he used as a target.

We had committed a cardinal error in bringing our family back to the United States for each child's senior year of high school. This is possibly the most difficult time for teenagers to adjust to a new school. For them, it was a year marked by loneliness and for their parents, by guilt.

Loneliness and an indifference to peer pressures are not uncommon among the "geographically mobile," as these youngsters are known in the shorthand of mental health researchers who interview, sample and analyze them in search of answers to questions like these:

Are mobile youngsters more prone to psychological disturbances than their rooted peers, or less? Does periodic moving have long-term consequences?

Most studies defy firm conclusions. At times, they flatly contradict one another. To the issue, for example, of how well mobile children perform in school, four studies say better than their domestic counterparts; six say about the same, and five say worse.

A 1993 study, completed for the State Department by the Ackerman Institute for Family Therapy in New York City, reviewed three decades of professional literature on the subject. Additionally, it studied in some depth 35 Foreign Service families.

The study found no significant psychological differences between mobile youngsters and their domestic counterparts. Moreover, it concluded that Foreign Service youngsters were in better shape than their guilt-ridden parents thought.

Still, they undergo problems with self-esteem, identity quandaries, social adjustments and fears, as do their rooted peers, but often with a difference. One colleague, for example, recalls his young daughter's asking as they were packing for a third overseas transfer, "Do we die if we stop moving?"

Dr. Sidney Werkman, a psychiatrist in Washington and a former State Department consultant, tends to give these conflicting findings a back seat to the critical question of what kind of character these youngsters will develop. While it is impossible, he says, to predict accurately how any child will turn out, there is considerable anecdotal evidence indicating that children raised abroad becoming members of a "third culture."

"Third culture people find their roots not in a neighborhood but in the international community that travels around the world and discovers meaning in shared interests instead of an accident of geography," he wrote in a 1977 book, "Bringing Up Children Overseas."

Dr. Werkman sees these youngsters as having an advantage over their rooted American peers. As the countries of the world become interdependent and the United States becomes more of a multi-ethnic society, he says, overseas youngsters move naturally and comfortably in this growing culture.

Despite this assurance, it can be wrenching to watch one's children return to American schools and find themselves out of place and out of touch. My older daughter had no knowledge of or interest in the lyrics of popular American music; she preferred tunes from Indian films. Her sister, rejecting fads and slang, buried herself in books for her school year.

Yet things did not always go smoothly in overseas schools either, as we discovered after one daughter had been in a French lycée for three months. My wife was called to a conference with the school director, who casually dismissed our daughter, then 8, as retarded because she had not yet spoken a word of French. Reluctantly, the director agreed to change the child's teacher, and, mysteriously, French began pouring from her mouth.

With each of our family's moves, my concerns remained. I wondered with my wife whether we had erred in choosing a career overseas; in all, we lived in six countries in nearly three decades. I wondered whether our family might benefit from counseling.

My wife, who took to life abroad with the zeal of a Marco Polo, thought it was my psyche alone that required counseling. By her reckoning, the children were doing just fine, which meant they weren't setting fire to cats, running away, rebelling any more than normal adolescents might.

Still, I worried, not so much about their stability but about their identity as Americans. I feared they would fail to develop the appreciation for their homeland with which I had grown up. This led me to use the dinner hour to counter the inclination of some of their teachers abroad to attribute blame for the world's ills to the United States.

For my efforts I became known to my children as "Mr. Super-American." This only fed my concern that they were failing to acquire an appreciation for America's freedoms, diversity and vitality.

In their temporary homes -- among them India for six years and Kenya for four -- they were exposed to extreme racial, ethnic and religious strife, poverty and sexual discrimination. I feared I was failing to get across that the United States at least struggles -- noisily -- against these ills.

It was while we were living in Paris in the late 70s that my concerns began to ease. It happened during dinner when my son turned up with a puffed lip from an exchange of blows with a French classmate. "He hit a boy who called him a stupid American," his sister said. "The other boy hit him first."

"Well," said my son, "I was getting tired of fellows who knock America and don't know what they're talking about. I shouldn't have hit him back, but what's a fellow to do."

"What is a fellow to do," my wife echoed.

I still wonder whether we did the right thing, not for the children but for my wife and me. Dr. Werkman estimates that two of every three geographically mobile youngsters pursue career paths that will take them back abroad.

Our son, a journalist, is assigned to New Delhi. The older daughter, an actress, works in London. The youngest is in law school in New York. She called the other day to let us know she has received a human rights internship for next summer in Cambodia. It's getting lonely at home.

Leonard L. Lefkow, who lives in Chevy Chase, Maryland, served 28 years in the Foreign Service.

TRAVELERS

by Beth Rambo

for the 1987 U.S. reunions of
Central School for Missionaries' Children and
The American School of Kinshasa, Zaire

Even those who've stopped in one place,
snug in Georgia, Saskatchewan, or
Indiana, are traveling. Night in Richmond, this one
dreams a steamship heaving across the grey
Atlantic. Pausing at the rocky, glaring Canaries,
he looks for yellow songsters, finds
seagulls, and sails on. He wakes up sobbing at Matadi
docks, and his wife turns, mumbles,
"What is it sweetheart?" and sleeps again.
Another, walking home in Denver: the first raindrops
splat on dry lawns and road, and the damp, dusty scent
takes her up, hurls her into Africa, end of dry season.
She breathes it in, in, and sighs it out.
Raises her umbrella, never explains.
Dry brown hyacinths on a Florida beach raise cliffs
for him, Moanda in moonlight, green water
turned muddy. One dreams a sentry's fire,
puffs the gourd water-pipe and coughs himself awake
muttering Tshiluba he's tried to forget.
Another swims upriver in her sleep, stroking
against the current, never moving forward. Voices warn
of crocodiles, and she laughs.
Some travel back, hoping
to find home. But even in Africa, you must make a place
for who you are now, not just your father's son,
your mother's daughter. Little time, now,
for rivers, trees, and animals that made your childhood
paradise. The jungle hides rebels; hungry, bored soldiers
block the roads; no parts for your car, nor medicines
for your patients' incurable diseases. . .

Grown up, you no longer find breakdown in a sandpit
amusing. You're old and strong enough now
to have to help dig it out.

We are still traveling,
even in the PTA, even as our children watch TV
cartoons or play with GI Joes, video games, Legos,
while a father remembers palmwood cars and helicopters,
hot afternoons in a high mango-tree clubhouse.
A mother remembers books by lanternlight,
and a small, clean monkey asleep, hugging her arm.
Would they give their children those things, if
they could? And would they send them away
to live and conspire and laugh with other children,
to cry alone, to be taught and mothered by others?

And some travel on
from state to state, country to country, leaving
friends and lovers, being left, and moving again.
They don't need to explain any more. Somewhere
Congo/Zaire merges with Kenya with Rhode Island
with Cote d'Ivoire with Louisiana with Belgium with
Vietnam. Now and then we meet and embrace, and let
go again.

When we come together, we form our own nation
of travelers, of in-betweens. Even where we've blended, stopped
trying to explain, we meet our own again and know
each other -- this one understands, we speak the same
memories; dream ourselves in the same overloaded truck
rattling and bumping along in a cloud of dust as we sing.

*Beth Rambo's parents first went to the Congo (now Zaire), Africa, as
medical missionaries (PCUSA) when she was ten. Ms. Rambo spent
grades 5-7 and 9-12 at the schools mentioned in the article above.
Currently, Ms. Rambo teaches English literature at Biola University, La
Mirada, California.*

GROWING UP INTERNATIONALLY MOBILE

By Julia Love

I was quite excited when I found out that we were moving to Germany. I was 11 years old, and really did not remember a lot about my earlier experience, seven years previously. There were, however, some things that would never leave my memory. I remember the old German man who lived in the house behind ours, and how he would give us candy all the time not just for a holiday. This was great especially since Halloween is not celebrated in Germany. I remember singing "London's Burning" in the British kindergarten, with a British accent. And I most vividly remember our big trip to England, and seeing Buckingham Palace and the Queen's jewels. Despite having only a few memories, I have heard many stories about my international childhood.

You can imagine how excited I was to find out that we were moving back to Germany. At the age of 11, moving around did not really affect me, I looked at moving as just another adventure. This was not true for my 14 year old sister. As a freshman cheerleader in a big Texas high school she was not too thrilled about moving overseas. Mom, who was also excited about our return to Europe, did her best to prepare us for the move. She even called the high school so that we would have an idea about the classes and activities. They did not have cheerleading, but she assured my sister that there would be a Prom. We talked a lot about the differences in the culture, what it would be like to go to an International School, and the changes we would all have to make. Sounded great to me, and so the adventure began.

The four years we spent in Germany were the best years, so far, in my life. Who ever would have thought that this American Army Brat would have become such an international person? The entire experience is one that will be a part of me forever. I will never forget the ski trip that our school had in February 1991, or that night that five of us stayed up for hours, talking about the Gulf War. It was so interesting listening to the views of one American, one British, one German, one Danish, and one Persian. I knew that these were friends that I would have for a long time.

It was so neat to walk down the halls in school and hear ten different languages being spoken. It was even neater to hear one person speaking one language, and then turn to another person and speak in a different language, and turn to another person and speak a third. Until moving to Germany, I spoke one language, English, with a strong Texas accent. All of those friends in Texas spoke one language as well, and were maybe studying a second. Even though I got used to hearing many different languages in the international school, I never took it for granted. I was constantly impressed and wished that I too would end up bilingual like my European friends.

It wasn't only the language capabilities of my friends in Hamburg that made me envious, but also their knowledge of world events and their beautiful style. I was determined to become as European as I could, and I set out to make the gradual change to internationalism. It wasn't hard since there were only four Americans in the class of 35 at the international school. It was easier for me to change and try to blend in than to hang on to my Americanism. I wasn't quite sure why I felt the need to shed some of my cultural identity and to try to take on another. Was I a superficial person or had I learned to live the life of a chameleon, changing to adapt to the environment? My mother had taught me to adapt to any situation in which I found myself. But had she created a monster? Had I been too quick to shed my American identity? Somehow I felt I did the only thing I could to really enjoy and live within another culture.

As with everything in life, all good things must come to an end, and we had to move back to the United States. I was in the middle of high school and the last thing I needed was to be uprooted and moved to a "foreign" country. I wasn't kidding, the United States seemed like a foreign country to me, and I did not want to go there. My sister had become a big part of my life and she was going to college. Not only was I embarking on an adventure that scared me to death, I was watching my sister leave home and start a new life in college.

Tears slowly filled my eyes as I watched my mother say goodbye to my sister in the doorway of her dorm room. It was then my turn to say goodbye, and as I embraced Halley, the tears poured down my cheeks. All the years we spent arguing and fighting seemed forgotten. All the dreams we shared and the time we spent together seemed more valuable than ever. At that moment I realized that I had taken our relationship for granted, she was not only my older sister, but also my best friend.

We had just moved back to the States after four years in Germany, and there were many changes we were all experiencing. Halley was going to college, and I was moving to a new place. It seemed like a foreign country to me, because I had changed so much in those four years. We all had. The American community in Hamburg was small, and my sister and I were forced to become closer friends than we would have been in the United States.

As I sat on her bed in her new dorm that day, I watched Halley and wondered what life would be like without her. I flipped through an old photo album she had brought with her. As I turned the pages looking at old birthday pictures, Christmas pictures, pictures of our trips to England, Italy, Turkey, and ski trips in the Alps, each picture made me stop and think. At that moment, I realized how lucky I had been and how much I have taken for granted the opportunities and experiences I have had. As I looked at our annual Christmas picture, taken on the top of a snowy mountain looking down one side into Switzerland and the other side into Italy, I thought how grateful I am for those experiences. At every turn of the page, I realized it was the experience that changed me.

Moving back to the United States was extremely difficult for me, and being away from Halley made it worse. I felt like I was that snowy mountain, one side of me American and the other side European. In Europe I was "the American," but in my own country I felt like a foreigner. Halley was the only person who understood what I was going through, yet she was so far from home. I wondered if we would grow apart, and I thought that I would never be able to share my feelings with anyone else. After all, we straddled that mountain together.

I never thought that the day we left Halley at her new home would be one of the saddest days of my life. Had I lost my best friend? How ridiculous - you never lose a sister and it is hard to find a better friend.

It was extremely hard those first six or seven months. I didn't really have any friends except one or two people who I ate lunch with. I made myself get involved in some activities but it didn't help much. I had missed the tryouts for the chorus, and I wasn't a super jock which was a prerequisite for any sport. At the international school if you knew what the basketball looked like, you could play on the team. And playing on the team meant road trips to other major European cities. I suppose I was glad I didn't have to deal with a boring American high school sports team. When would I ever get a grip on the situation that was ruining my life?

The answer to that question came when I tried out for the spring musical and got a part. I suddenly was no longer an outsider. I had an identity and I had a name people knew. Those awful months of feeling so alone and so weird were over, just like that. I knew I had grown from the experience because that's what I had always heard would happen.

The experience was something my grandfather would say was character building. He was the one who started this whole third culture kid thing in the first place by taking my mother to Austria when she was two years old. It has been hard and it has been fun and I wouldn't trade my life for anything. Growing up internationally mobile is something only those of us who have done it can understand. It is like a secret and special club with an initiation that you can't explain. It is a way of life that never leaves you, no matter where you live. It is in your blood, and it becomes a part of you, and you pass it on to your kids if they are lucky.

Julia Marks Love was 18 and a senior at George Mason High School when she wrote "Growing Up Internationally Mobile." Ms. Love lived in German communities in Landsberg, Münster, and Hamburg, Germany during eight years of her childhood with her military family. An International Baccalaureate candidate, she graduated in June 1994 and will attend St. Lawrence University in Canton, New York.

PARENTING INTERNATIONALLY:
Tools You Can Give Your Mobile Children to Help Them Thrive

by Anne-Marie Atkinson, LCSW-C

It's afternoon, and the sun is about to slip down behind the hills of the Swiss Jura. My bedroom is a mess because I am having a hard time making up my mind exactly what to take to college in the trunk I'm trying to pack. The college did send a list of suggested items to bring, but I know from experience such lists don't always reflect what I'm really going to need. I know this not because I have ever been to college before (at this point I haven't), but because I've spent a lot of time packing for unfamiliar places -- I've grown up in a Foreign Service family. Still, such lists can be helpful, so, from a perspective many years removed from that afternoon in the messy bedroom, here's my "top ten" list of things to pack for your children as you prepare for an international move.

1. An interest in ADVENTURE. The one thing you can guarantee is that the new place is going to be different from the old place. Encourage your children to wonder, question, and explore in age-appropriate ways. Model for them an interest in new activities and an openness to other ways of thinking and doing: that doesn't mean abandoning cherished values -- it does mean giving your children the chance to learn from the richness of human experience, and developing in them the ability to live in harmony with those who are different from themselves (the root of world peace). The challenges your child faces will change over the years, but the ability to explore and adapt with grace and flexibility will stand them in good stead whether they are negotiating with a spouse or a business colleague, entering a new school or beginning a new career.

2. As much CONTROL as possible over the move. It is disconcerting to have your familiar world vanish every few years. The more control your children feel they have over that disconcerting experience, the

86

more secure they will be in general. Even small children can choose which of several toys to bring. Parents will make the final decision about which apartment to rent, but asking children for their comments can include them in the decision-making process in an appropriate way. Giving your children as much practice as possible in making CHOICES now will also protect them in later years, when the choices they will <u>have</u> to make will have increasingly serious consequences.

3. The opportunity to say GOODBYE. That means telling children about the move in advance, and encouraging them to think through how, when, and to whom they want to say goodbye. It may include a formal farewell walk through the neighborhood (complete with camera), a party, or a series of get-togethers with favorite friends. Saying goodbye includes acknowledging the good things you'll remember, as well as any regrets you may have; trying to resolve or reconcile remaining problems (rather than just escaping them by getting on that plane), and sharing hopes for the future.

Children should also be offered the chance to MAINTAIN CONTACT with people important to them. Yes, they will make new friends, but each old friend is still a unique individual who will be missed. Writing letters, exchanging drawings or photographs, and short long-distance phone calls are all ways to keep in touch. Other adults -- relatives, parents of friends, neighbors -- can be a wonderful resource for your children, as they teach them how to tap dance (you never learned) or provide a Thanksgiving haven for your college student when you are overseas. Help your child build and maintain those relationships.

4. Another way to give control is to give your children the KNOWLEDGE that TRANSITION is an understandable emotional PROCESS: there are certain stages that almost everyone's feelings and behavior go through. Help your children think about where they are in the process, and talk with them about what they might expect during the next stages. The movers will prepare your furniture for the move. It is up to you to prepare your child's feelings.

5. Permission to GRIEVE and express ANGER appropriately. The gifts your children will gain from their international moves are very

real -- and so is the pain of loss they will feel. Allow your children to articulate their sadness, even their anger, at the disruption in their lives. Loss is part of every life -- in acknowledging their losses and allowing your children to grieve, you will be giving them the opportunity to learn how to face loss and pain, and move beyond it in a positive way.

6. TRANSFERABLE SKILLS and COMMON FAMILY INTERESTS are also important. Your child can enjoy swimming or music by a Swedish lake or a Tunisian beach. Hiking in Switzerland was quite different from walking in Greece, but the fun our family enjoyed on those treks still inspires me to roust out my own family for a stroll in the Shenandoah. Skills and interests are also a good way to meet people in a new place -- for adults and children.

7. PEERS. Make sure your child has the opportunity to talk to or spend time with other internationally mobile children. This can be especially important in the United States, where school classmates may have known each other since kindergarten, don't understand why you are really good at soccer but haven't a clue about football, or may resent your criticism of Ski Roundtop ("after the Alps? PUHLEEZE").

8. It is crucial to include FAMILIAR OBJECTS in your shipment, and to develop consistent FAMILY ROUTINES and rituals that can be maintained wherever you are. Our Christmas tree varied from a Douglas fir to a Thai silver-paper one, but it always wore the same ornaments. The bed your child sleeps in may change, but it could be covered with the same spread. Bedtime might include teeth brushing, a story, and a big hug wherever you are.

Encourage your children to keep a SCRAP BOOK, a diary, or a special box of mementos. After a few moves, the past can start to feel pretty chaotic, and you can even start to wonder if some event really happened (since you may be the only one around who remembers the day you and your friend fell in that klong, and even the klong is on the other side of the world now). The concrete documentation of a scrap book or a memento can help your child organize, remember and tell his own story, which will also help with that all-important question, "Who am I?"

9. Give your children an internationally mobile role model: tell them about the concept of a THIRD CULTURE KID (TCK)/Global Nomad.

(According to David Pollock, you are a TCK "if you have spent a significant part of your developmental years in a culture other than your parents' culture, developing a sense of relationship to all of those cultures while not having full ownership in any. Elements from each culture are incorporated into your life, but your sense of belonging is in relationship to others of similar experience.") Some famous global nomads include John Denver, Henry Luce, Pearl Buck and Nobel Peace Prize winner Daw Aung San Suu Kyi.

Encourage your children to develop a picture of their own particular "third culture," from favorite foods to dress codes to philosophies of life. You can help by talking to them about your own values and tastes, and encouraging them to express their own preferences as appropriate. The more a child is aware of and secure in who she is, the more resistant she will be to being led astray by other people's pressure.

If your child complains he can't find a name or a category for himself that he is comfortable with, encourage him to create his own. A man I know, who grew up in Canada and the United States, now identifies himself as a "North American." I've accepted that to make my favorite dinner I need to visit both an Asian grocery store and a French bakery. Another friend, blonde and blue-eyed, removes the discreet Indian diamond from her pierced nose when she is going to her law office, but she does wear it to parties on weekends.

You can also help by accepting your children as who they are. Just as your child may be different from you because she is learning about computers in kindergarten or he prefers Barney to Yogi Bear, an internationally mobile child is going to be different from a parent who grew up moving around the American Midwest or who lived in the same house until high school. You still have many wonderful things in common, and your children still need and value your attention and leadership (no matter what they say on a particular day!). A child who knows his parent loves him as he is, is a child who can love both himself and others.

10. And finally, don't forget to USE all these TOOLS WHEN RE-ENTERING the United States! You may be coming home and can relax into the familiar, but for your children "home" may be the post you just left. Encourage them to approach life in the U.S. in the same

spirit of adventure as a new post. Using these tools on your way to Dulles airport as well as to l'aerodrome Charles de Gaulle can help ensure a smooth transition for everyone.

Happy traveling!

P.S. Even if you decide to stop being an internationally mobile family, there are still two tools every parent should keep handy.

The first is a basic knowledge of normal human development. That will help you sleep at night, as you will be able to put your child's behavior into context (both toddlers and teens tend to say "no" with some frequency, for example -- it's not necessarily a reaction to you personally!). That information will also help you decide when your child may need some extra help. You will know that a five-year old who can't read is perfectly normal, but an eight-year old who can't may be cause for concern.

The second tool is a working knowledge of some basic parenting techniques, such as appropriate limit setting at different ages. You may have been lucky enough to learn all you need to know from your own parents, but if you didn't, then read, watch parenting TV shows or other parents, or take a class. Your investment will pay off in more pleasurable parenting.

Some good parenting books: The New Peoplemaking (Virginia Satir), Playground Politics: Understanding the Emotional Life of Your School-Age Child (Stanley Greenspan), Positive Discipline (Jane Nelson), and How to Talk So Kids Will Listen & Listen So Kids Will Talk (Adele Faber & Elaine Mazlish).

Anne-Marie Atkinson, LCSW-C, is a clinical social worker and parent who grew up in Southeast Asia and Europe as a member of a Foreign Service family. She is married to a global nomad and works as a writer, trainer and clinician with cross-cultural children and families.

QUITO

by Robb Mack

The thousands of lights
stating the future
in a new world so different
yet so unique in itself
surrounded by walls of darkness
to keep the outside world away, a
world that seems so distant, from
wandering eyes, and straining ears,
straining for sounds not linked to the future
but a sound that comes from the real world
that can be related as good.

The feeling of having to belong here belongs somewhere else,
and the little feeling of home comes from his last memory of
his world left behind, the home in which he molded his life.
Now this mold must be forgotten, torn down, broken up,
so that the pieces be picked up and rebuilt in this new
surrounding, adding to pieces that seem appropriate, discarding
others that don't fit into the smooth round curve of the future.

*Robb Mack was 16 when he wrote "Quito." He was born in Brazil and
lived in Portugal, El Salvador, Paraguay and Ecuador during his
childhood. He graduated from Brewster Academy and is attending
Presbyterian College in South Carolina.*

SAFE KIDS, INVOLVED PARENTS:
The Power of Parent, School, and Community
Cooperation in the International Setting

by Joel Wallach and Gale A. Metcalf

Challenges of Raising Children Overseas

Being a parent anywhere is not easy. Being a parent overseas brings with it unique challenges as well as opportunities. For most children raised overseas, the benefits seem to outweigh the drawbacks. Compared to their peers back home, they seem better able to deal with cultural and racial differences. They develop a broader world view, seeing issues in terms of various shades of grey rather than as black or white (Cottrell, 1993). They also have the potential to develop closer relationships with their parents and siblings (Useem & Downie, 1976).

Growing up overseas, however, is not an unmitigated blessing. Children with physical or emotional disabilities may find that overseas schools and communities have limited resources to meet their needs. Reentry, and the attendant identity issues, can be a source of stress, especially after being away from the U.S. for an extended period (Werkman, 1979; Wallach & Metcalf, 1980, Piet-Pelon, 1986).

Those who decide to raise their children abroad quite naturally ask themselves, "How is the overseas lifestyle and environment different from 'back home' and what do I as a parent need to know?" It has become quite clear that raising children overseas creates some different and added demands on parents. Some of the more critical ones include:

1. *Helping Children Cope with Transition.* The overseas setting is a transient one. If your child is not the newcomer, then he or she often is about to lose his or her best friend. This teaches youngsters who grow up overseas valuable social skills for connecting quickly with others. For some children, it also may work against the development of skills needed to maintain long-term intimate relationships (Werkman, Farley, Butler & Quayhagen, 1981). Extroverts thrive in the overseas environment; introverts may have more difficulty.

Another effect of the transient overseas environment is that the nuclear family becomes the "anchor," the source of stability in a changing environment. On the positive side, this means that children raised overseas often are close to and communicate well with their parents, even during adolescence. On the negative side, they may have a harder time breaking away from a supportive family and finding their independence as they go on to college or independent living.

2. *Teaching Children Responsibility.* Many overseas environments can put children (and quite often non-working spouses) in a more dependent role than they are accustomed to back home. With children, this can make the issue of teaching responsibility more difficult. As a result, teaching responsibility is an issue which requires special emphasis in the overseas setting. For example, because of legal, language and cultural constraints, teens who might take jobs after school or during the summer when in the U.S. often find these possibilities restricted overseas. Household help, available in many countries, can limit opportunities for children to learn responsibility through sharing in household chores. Furthermore, it is easy for parents to feel guilty for bringing their children overseas. This can quickly and easily translate into permissive or rescuing behavior, at times when children need to face the consequences of their actions (Wallach & Metcalf, 1982).

3. *Setting Limits.* International communities encompass a wide diversity of values and beliefs about what is and what is not appropriate behavior for children. Whether the issue is at what age alcohol consumption is permissible or what is an appropriate allowance for a 10-year-old, this value spectrum is likely to be broader than that which exists within most of our back home communities. As a result, parents may find that standards of acceptable behavior, especially for teens, vary widely from family to family.

Being new in an overseas community adds some special challenges with regard to setting limits. Parents often don't know which situations are safe for their children and which are not -- Where can they go? What can they do? How can they get there safely? Frequently, parents are asked to make decisions soon after their arrival at the new location, decisions for which they have limited background information. Also, they are often torn between wanting their children to make friends and be accepted, yet at the same time, wanting to ensure that they as parents provide limits which help ensure their children's safety.

In many overseas posts, particularly in third world countries, the local police may be reluctant to get involved with expatriate youth, especially children of diplomats. If police turn a blind eye, it is easy for youngsters to feel that they are "above the law." this means that, unlike back home, risk-taking youth often can go quite far before host country law enforcement will intervene. It also means that setting limits, first and foremost a parental responsibility, becomes even more significant in the overseas environment where parents and the school become the primary, and often only, monitors of youth behavior.

Recent research (Rodgers, 1993) indicates that American teens abroad participate in "at risk" behavior such as smoking cigarettes, drinking alcohol, and using other drugs, at about the same levels as their peers back home. In essence, American teenagers, whether at home or abroad, function first and foremost like American teenagers, at least when it comes to some types of "at risk" behavior.

In any group of youngsters, there always will be a small percentage of serious risk-takers -- those who will push the limits as far as they can, no matter what. Equivalently, there also will be a minority who will never get into trouble, no matter how easy it might be or what inducements are set before them. Then, of course, there is the vast middle. This is the group that can be swayed under certain circumstances to undertake risky behavior, such as drinking, using other drugs, or participating in vandalism. It has been our experience that key factors which can move this middle group towards high risk behaviors include the presence of a charismatic leader engaging in the behavior, the absence of parental and community limits and the lack of attractive, healthy alternatives. After the children in the middle begin to move into the high risk-taking group, it becomes very difficult for parents to reestablish norms of appropriate behavior and to regain control. For example, after taking drugs, or staying out all night, or going to bars for weekend entertainment becomes the norm for the average teen in any community, it becomes very difficult to change that standard of behavior. On a community level, it is important to "keep the middle in the middle," and to provide intervention and support services for the risk-takers.

The Overseas Environment: Some Unique Assets

While providing some special challenges, the overseas setting offers unique assets to assist parents in raising their children. Many of the most serious problems affecting youth back home -- poverty, violence and racism -- are not problems for expatriate youth in overseas schools and communities. The small size of the international youth community often allows for problems to be spotted early. Most overseas schools provide a standard of education equal to, or better than, schools in our back home communities. They usually are staffed by committed and involved educators who often see the school as a center of life for children abroad. Generally, parents abroad are involved and concerned about the education and behavior of their children. All of this translates into an ideal laboratory setting in which parents, schools and communities, working together, can establish and/or maintain healthy standards of behavior for youth, with a degree of influence far beyond that which is possible back home.

A Case Study: Changing Standards of Teen Behavior in Taipei

One example of a successful parent, school and community intervention occurred in Taipei, Taiwan in 1992. Teachers and guidance counselors at Taipei American School began to notice an alarming increase in the lack of supervision of teens, unchaperoned parties and sleepovers, alcohol consumption and attendance at bars and discos by students of the American School in ninth and tenth grades and even some in grade eight. It seemed only a matter of time before someone was going to get hurt.

Taipei is a fast-paced, high stress Asian city. Many parents of expatriate youth are busy with demanding jobs, long commutes and, increasingly, with regional responsibilities which take them off-island for days or weeks at a time. As in many international communities, students in Taipei are able to purchase alcohol easily and the availability of cheap and plentiful taxi transportation opens the whole city to teens. While drinking and attendance at bars and discos traditionally had been the preserve of 11th and 12th graders, the same behavior at younger grade levels gave cause for concern.

Spearheaded by the school's PTA and the Community Services Center*, parents, school staff and community leaders decided to try to change the norms before the situation reached crisis proportions. The first step was to gather accurate information. Numbers of teens were surveyed in focus groups to explore the issues and hear their perspectives and concerns. Out of this, a survey was developed and administered to all 8th and 9th graders at the School. This survey focused on such issues as alcohol and other drug use, curfews, use of taxis and weekend activities. Results, when compared with similar surveys undertaken in previous years, indicated that the norms, indeed, were changing, with more youth going to bars and discos on weekends, greater alcohol consumption and more parents leaving their young teens unsupervised for longer periods.

At the same time, multiple meetings sponsored by the PTA and Community Services Center were held with parents to elicit their concerns and ideas for dealing with free time and setting limits for their children. Input also was solicited from teachers, guidance staff, school administrators and others in the community such as pastors and community youth workers. Consensus began to emerge that there was the potential for serious problems as the norms for teens in general, and 8th and 9th graders in particular, were beginning to change in directions that most parents, and many students, felt were not healthy for children or for the community.

A concerted community effort was undertaken to reverse these trends with a particular focus on pushing experimentation with alcohol back to later ages when, it was felt, those who decided to experiment would have a better chance of making responsible decisions and would be less likely to get themselves into serious difficulties. Intervention efforts included:

> (*The Community Services Center is a non-profit organization dedicated to fostering the well-being of the international community through mental health, educational and social service programs.)

1. *Parent Education*:

   -- A series of parent meetings were conducted in which parents were able to talk with each other about their concerns and learn about rules and guidelines in other families;

   -- A regularly scheduled program at the beginning of each school year for parents of 9th graders that addressed the special issues of raising children overseas and the special issues of parenting in Taipei was instituted;

   -- A regularly scheduled Spring program for 8th grade parents to discuss the changes coming with high school was instituted;

-- A range of parent education workshops and seminars were conducted throughout the year to address issues such as family communication, helping children deal with peer pressure, and steps parents can take to prevent alcohol and other drug abuse in their families;

-- A structured discussion program, "Parents and Teens Talking," was held. Parents had the opportunity to hear the concerns of teens (not their own!) and vice-versa;

-- A series of community-sponsored "Disco Tours" were offered. These brought parents to the most popular discos frequented by teens. This helped parents to make an informed decision as to whether these establishments were acceptable or not for their children.

2. *Prevention and Early Intervention*:

One of the best ways to deal with youth issues early is through effective prevention efforts. The School already had two prevention programs in place -- the School's health program and the School's Peer Counseling Program. These programs helped to reinforce and support efforts undertaken by parents and other community groups.

The School's health program, developed in recent years, placed special emphasis on issues of alcohol use and abuse. Importantly, it addressed the critical issues of resisting peer pressure and making responsible decisions. In addition, the School, in conjunction with the Community Services Center, had developed a peer counseling program in the high school. Through this program, students, chosen by the student body as natural listeners and problem-solvers, were trained in helping skills. This program was designed to reach those in need early through peer intervention and to facilitate referral to school and community professionals. In this instance, this program provided a direct avenue to reach teens as well as an effective vehicle to monitor the pulse of the youth community on issues of concern.

The few students at risk of developing serious problems were identified and, with the support of the School, interventions were made by professional counselors. Individual and family counseling was offered to the relief of a small number of families who felt they were losing control.

3. *Alternative Programs for Youth*

At the same time that parent education and youth intervention efforts were undertaken, it was recognized that the number of attractive, "healthy" activities for young teens on weekends was limited. A separate initiative was undertaken to develop alternative recreational activities that would appeal to 8th and 9th graders. A group composed of community secular and religious youth workers, along with a representative sample of teens, met to explore the needs and to define what could compete with the allure of flashy bars and discos. The outcome was the development of a teen-driven community youth program that focused on fun weekend activities (i.e., sports, supervised sleepovers, camping) that appealed to the younger teen group.

4. *Community Guidelines for Youth*

One clear message that came out of meetings with parents was the difficulty parents faced in knowing what were appropriate limits to set for their children, especially if they were new to the community. Questions such as:" "How late should a 14 year old stay out?" "Should teenage girls take taxis at night?" "How much allowance is appropriate for a 13 year old in this community?" were not easy for newcomers to answer. If limits are set too liberally initially, they are very difficult to retract. It was felt that a written set of community guidelines would help parents new to the community to have a reference point in making the critical decisions required early-on in their stay. Although parents might decide to deviate from the guidelines, at least they would have a beginning point for evaluating the rules they set for their children. Through guidelines, a sense of the risks, as perceived by other members of the community, could be communicated.

A community consensus process was undertaken to canvass parents and school staff on what the critical issues were that needed to be included, not only for 8th and 9th graders, but for all teens in the community. That Spring, a series of meetings were conducted with school guidance staff, community youth workers, parents and students. After much debate, discussion and compromise, a consensus document emerged. The Guidelines were approved by the school administration and the PTA. The following Fall, they were distributed by the PTA in both English and Chinese versions to all parents of students grades 8-12. Now the Guidelines are given by the School to all newly-registering parents of students in the 8th grade and the high school. They are also mailed each Fall by the PTA to all 8th and 9th grade parents.

All of this activity was begun in the Spring of 1992 and fully implemented during the 1992-93 school year. As of this writing (April, 1994), parents and school staff report that there has been a significant decrease in the attendance of 8th and 9th grade students at local discos and, in general, an increase in their participation in healthy, alternative activities. In addition, there is a heightened parental awareness of the need for limits for teens, a greater ease in parents talking with other parents about rules and limits for their children and a general rolling back of weekend curfews for young teens to earlier hours.

Making the Parent-School-Community Partnership Work

The Taipei international community's experience in reversing a potentially dangerous trend among youth clearly demonstrates that parents can make a difference overseas. Even a small group of concerned parents working together can change community norms. This is especially true when they join forces with the school staff and other community organizations in a concerted effort to introduce change. To maximize chances of success in instituting community change:

1. *Do your homework.* Research the issues so you know the depth and extent of the concern. Speak with school administrators, counselors, teachers and other parents. Do not rely on rumors to guide you.

2. *Build consensus.* Get as many people involved as possible. Form coalitions of school staff, parents and community leaders. Get youth involved and participating from the outset. Start by talking one-on-one to significant opinion leaders in both the adult and youth communities.

Suggested Guidelines for Parents
of Taipei American School Teens, Grades 8-12*

(Prepared by the PTA of Taipei American School and the
Community Services Center)

1. ***Talk with your teen*** clearly about your values,
   expectations and family rules regarding drinking, other drug
   use and sexual behavior.

2. ***Set clear, enforceable limits for your teen:***
   Consistently apply appropriate consequences for breaking
   family rules;
   Be sure the consequences are ones you are truly willing to
   enforce;
   Be open to negotiating your rules as your teen gets older and
   proves to be responsible and trustworthy.

3. ***Have a curfew.***

   Compare notes with the parents of your teen's friends and
   set a curfew that is right for your teen and your family's
   values. We suggest the following for your consideration:

   School nights (Sunday - Thursday) --
   Unless there is a special reason to be at school (i.e., band
   concert, sports practice) or another place, teens should be
   home by the time the 4:45 pm late bus arrives and should
   stay home on school nights.

   Weekend evenings (Friday - Saturday) --
8th graders	9:30 - 10:00 pm
9th graders	10:00-10:30 pm
10th graders	10:30 - 11:00 pm
11th graders	11:30 - 12:00 am
12th graders	12:00 - 1:00 am

4. *Monitor your teen's unsupervised time.*

Going out:

-- When your teen is going out, be sure you know where he or she is going;

-- If your teen is going to different locales, ask him or her to check with you periodically;

-- If plans change, ask your teen to call and let you know where he or she will be. Get a telephone number, so you can reach your teen.

Sleepovers:

-- When your teen is invited to spend the night, call to find out if the parents will be home and what time the family expects their teen (and yours) to be in the house.

Parties:

-- When your teen is invited to a party, call the host parent and ask what adult supervision there will be.

-- If you do not allow your teen to drink, state this rule and ask if alcohol will be served.

When you leave town:

-- Do not leave your teen alone or with a housekeeper. This practice potentially places your teen (and your housekeeper) under tremendous pressure for your home to become a party place. It is better to arrange for your teen to stay with another family or for another adult to stay with your teen in your home.

5. *Money/Allowances*:

Having too much money can cause problems for teens. It is difficult to set an allowance applicable to all students. However, it seems reasonable to estimate most high school students need $20 per week to cover snacks, one meal out at a fast food restaurant and non-school transportation. Beyond this, determining the amount of spending money depends on what else the allowance is to cover (i.e., lunches, school supplies, weekend entertainment).

6. *Make discos, pubs and beer halls off limits for your 8th or 9th grade teen.*

   The atmosphere which exists in these establishments is not appropriate for 8-9th graders. This is not to say that these establishments are appropriate for older teens. That is a decision you can best make by visiting these places yourself and determining their suitability for your older teen.

7. Many teens use taxis to get around Taipei. Taxis are relatively safe in the daytime and when taken in groups. **Teens, particularly girls, are strongly advised against using taxis alone in the evenings.**

8. Motorcycles are dangerous! In Taiwan, you must be 18 years old and have a Taiwan license to legally drive a motorcycle of any size. **If your teen drives or rides on a motorcycle, insist that he or she wear a helmet.**

(*Each community will have different concerns and needs. The Guidelines presented above address the specific priority issues and conditions in the Taipei community.)

3. *Share ownership.* Work behind the scenes to get existing community or school groups/leaders to take responsibility for and to promote ideas for change.

4. *Address the issues on a number of fronts.* A multi-faceted approach from a number of directions is likely to promote longer-term, substantive changes.

5. *Think long-term.* Youth communities go through cycles -- periods in which everything seems to be going well followed by more difficult times. While the specific concerns may have been catalyzed by an incident or crisis and immediate attention is required, efforts are most profitably directed towards long-term solutions. Prevention works.

6. *Institutionalize change.* Whenever possible, encourage existing groups (the school, PTA, youth programs, etc.) to take ownership for new programs or initiatives. This way, any changes are likely to be maintained after a committed individual or group is reassigned and leaves the community.

7. *Help parents support parents.* Devise strategies that facilitate parents talking and supporting each others. This is especially important for parents new to the community. Create opportunities for both formal and informal communication among parents.

8. *Don't be afraid of taking a stand.* Although it is easier to sit back, do nothing, and await your next transfer, it is worth your while to speak up. Your voice has great potential to be heard in the overseas community. Parents <u>can</u> make a difference.

References

Cottrell, A.B. (1993, November). ATCKs have problems relating to own ethnic groups. <u>Newslinks, XIII</u> (2), pp. 1, 4.

Piet-Pelon, N. (1986, June). Reentry for teens. <u>Foreign Service Journal</u>, pp. 28-30.

Rodgers, Thomas A. (1993, October). Here are findings on how American teens behave overseas. <u>Foreign Service Journal</u>, pp. 20-24.

Useem, R.H., and Downie, R.D. (1976, September/October). Third-culture kids. <u>Today's Education</u>, pp. 103-105.

Wallach, J. and Metcalf, G.A. (1980, Winter). The hidden problem of reentry. <u>The Bridge</u>, pp. 29-30.

Wallach, J. and Metcalf, G.A. (1982, June). Parenting abroad. <u>Foreign Service Journal</u>, pp. 20-23.

Werkman, S.L. (1979). Coming home: Adjustment problems of adolescents who have lived overseas. In S.C. Feinstein & P.L. Giovacchini (Eds.) <u>Adolescent Psychiatry (Vol. 7): Developmental and Clinical Studies</u>, pp. 175-190. Chicago. University of Chicago Press.

Werkman, S.L., Farley, G.K., Butler, C., and Quayhagen, M. (1981). The psychological effects of moving and living overseas. <u>Journal of the American Academy of Child Psychiatry</u>, pp. 645-657.

Joel Wallach and Gale Metcalf are the Co-Directors of the Community Services Center of Taipei, Taiwan. The Community Services Center is a community-based, non-profit organization closely affiliated with Taipei American School, providing mental health, social service, and educational programs to the international community of Taipei. Wallach and Metcalf have worked as guidance consultants to international schools and to the U.S. State Department for the last 16 years. They have run school-based prevention programs at Cairo American College, the International School of Kuala Lumpur, and Taipei American School.

COMING HOME:
A Difficult Decision

by Adrienne Benson

[Reprinted with permission from the April 1988 issue of
The Foreign Service Journal.]

The fact that I've grown up in Africa, outside my own culture, is
valuable to me. Roasting mangoes in the vacant lot, creating a three-
ring circus using elite termites, and listening to lions roar through the
night as I lay with my family in our VW bus are all treasured
memories of my childhood. Africa, for children, is a sort of utopia, a
paradise of open spaces, wild animals, and an incredible diversity of
people and places. I would never trade my experiences as a child in
Africa, but deciding to return to the United States for boarding school
as a high school junior was the best and hardest decision I have ever
made.

In Nairobi, the excitement I had felt one summer vacationing in
Europe refused to subside. The bubble of Eden I had once imagined
Africa to be suddenly seemed tired and restricting; I yearned for more.
I was tired of sitting in my room and listening to music or wandering
the drab streets of Nairobi with my friends. I knew there was more to
life than waking up in the morning feeling angry and rebellious,
brushing off my family with curt remarks and sour looks. I began to
strongly feel a need to connect with my own culture, to test its
freedoms and explore its offerings. I began to discuss the possibility
of returning to the United States for my last two years of high school.

My parents understood my need to expand my horizons, but urged me
to think carefully, go slowly, and make sure I was doing the right
thing. The week before my cultural anthology class embarked on our
eight-day field study of the Maasai tribe, my grandmother called and
suggested that I should look into attending boarding school. The next
few days were probably the most confusing and distressing of my life.
I would burst into tears at the slightest provocation and then suddenly
be over the rooftops with joy at the prospect of going to America to
live. My grandmother's phone call came at the perfect time because it
gave me eight days of living in the quiet Maasai village and trekking
through the forest to think, to weigh my options.

On the last day of the Maasai expedition, my class hiked all morning to reach the bus. We were sitting on a rocky hill overlooking an expanse of striking Kenyan scenery. Below us herds of Thompson's gazelle and zebras grazed on the gold grass. Long-tailed widow birds flitted awkwardly, tails dragging about the bushes. "If I were a Maasai, I would be satisfied with the beauty of Kenya and the simplicity of life, but I am not. I am an American who has spent most of my life in Africa. My future, however, is in my own country." I felt very relieved and comfortable with my decision to return to the United States. Bouncing over the rutted dirt roads on the trip back to Nairobi, I was relaxed and serene.

Months later, after I had exchanged tearful good-byes with all of my Nairobi friends, I stood in front of my new American school's main building, hugging my parents good-bye. I was upset at the prospect of them leaving, and suddenly unsure of whether I had made the right decision. My new school and home seemed so imposing, and all of the students so sure of themselves. For the first time, I was alone with my longed-for adventure.

Now in my second and last year at boarding school, I realize how happy I am. I have grown infinitely in the last year and am growing still, every day. Now cities are all around me: Baltimore, Philadelphia, Washington, D.C. I am no longer surprised at the openness of people in their attitudes toward the government; in fact I've taken part in political rallies myself -- something I never thought I'd have a chance to do. In the last year at boarding school I've almost become a different person, much more open and satisfied with my surroundings and myself -- especially myself. Boarding school isn't the right choice for everyone; I have seen people come to my new school, feel miserable, and then leave, not taking or giving anything. But I made an important decision and came out for the best -- far better than I thought I would and much better than if I hadn't taken the risk at all.

Growing up as a Foreign Service dependent outside of America has given me a more open view of the world. I've experienced different cultures, traditions, and views of life. I feel I'm a more accepting and open-minded person because of my experiences.

Returning to the United States, however, was, at this point in my life, the wisest decision I've made. I have access to the best of both worlds now: the openness, freedom, and opportunity of America and the diversity, warmth, and beauty of Africa.

Adrienne Benson was 17, a senior at Westtown School in Pennsylvania when she wrote this article. She had lived in Africa for ten years, in Zambia, Kenya, Liberia, and the Ivory Coast. Ms. Benson went on to receive a Bachelor of Arts degree in English (with honors) from Lewis and Clark College in Portland, Oregon. After graduation, she joined the Peace Corps, currently serving as a PCV English teacher in Nepal.

COMING IN FOR A LANDING
How Families Can Prepare for the
Rude Shock of Returning Home

by Eugenia E. Gratto

[Reprinted with permission from the September 1990 issue of
The Foreign Service Journal.]

Reentry. In space flights, it's a dangerous process, one in which the
craft is at a high risk of burning up as it comes in contact with the
Earth's atmosphere. It takes more than skill for a pilot to maneuver
the ship safely. In many ways, reentry to the United States is the same
for a Foreign Service child or teenager.

I was three years old when my family moved to Bonn for our first
overseas assignment. When I was seven, we moved to Madrid, and
when I was 10, we moved to Lagos. I moved back to Virginia for
eighth grade, and moving back to the States was a horrible experience
for me. It took me almost two years to get really comfortable and
settled in to American life. Almost every Foreign Service kid I talk to
says the same thing. I'd like to give parents some advice on making
your kid's reentry a little smoother and also describe a little about what
I wish I'd known.

For the parents

Let your children watch TV. Television, as a medium, dominates
American life. TV can be useful for kids new to the States because it
helps them get more in touch with fashions, slang, attitudes, and other
bits of pop culture. It may seem to parents like they are advocating
brain rot, but in the long run, it will really help.

Get your children into AWAL. "Around the World in a Lifetime,"
coordinated through the State Department's Family Liaison Office, is
an incredibly useful support/social group that can make the transition
easier by putting Foreign Service kids in the Washington, D.C. area in
touch with one another. I felt very alone when I came back, because I
couldn't find anyone else like me. AWAL can help combat that
feeling.

Let them cry. Don't let them bottle up their feelings. I cried almost every night for my first five or six months back, and it made me feel a little better.

Don't say you understand. The fact is, you don't. For the Foreign Service employee, there are people at work who have similar experiences and will accept a new colleague quickly. For the spouse, there are old friends from the neighborhood, a new job -- to sum it up, there are mature adults around to talk to. Kids are not as mature or accepting, and they may be rejecting your child at school. Your kids may go through social hell; and there's nothing anyone can do about it. Be understanding, but realize that that doesn't mean that you know what it's like.

Don't paint an unreal picture of life in the United States. Remember, you have been out of the country just as long as they have, maybe even longer, and you're just as out of touch with it as they are.

Don't let your own feelings be hurt. When my parents moved me back to the States, I was very angry. I'm sure they knew exactly how I felt, because I wasn't very subtle about it. Don't let this get to you. Your kids are just displacing their loneliness and anger and throwing it at you because you're the closest people to them. Remember that it's not anyone's fault, and it's especially not yours. It will pass, and things will get better, but give them lots of time.

As for the kids

Read the tips for your parents!

Join AWAL. It's fun, and it can really help when you need someone to talk to who knows what you're talking about.

Don't broadcast where you've lived. Get some friends, get your foothold in the school, and don't tell everyone about your life experiences. Don't lie about them, but don't talk about them too much. They may not understand. In my case the students had no way to relate to me because I was coming from such a different world.

Try not to blame your parents. This one's really hard, but believe me, they're not trying to hurt you. They love you, and they want to help you get through the adjustment. If you fight that, it'll make it worse.

Keep smiling (or at least try to). If you walk around with an angry or sullen expression on your face, no one will like you. Trust me. Smile and act friendly. People will be nicer to you that way.

Remember, it's going to get better. If you just hang in there, you'll figure out that the States aren't quite so bad. Maybe it'll be when you're at the mall bumming around with your new friends. You will eventually feel like you're home. Just give yourself time, and you'll make it.

Living overseas is an incredibly enriching experience for a child of any age. Experiences, friends, and exposure to many cultures helps cultivate an open mind and often higher maturity. Yes, there are great advantages to being a Foreign Service kid. Just don't come back to the States completely unprepared for what may be ahead.

Ms. Gratto lived in Germany, Spain and Nigeria during her childhood. In 1989-90, she served as teen coordinator of Around the World in a Lifetime. She graduated from Mary Baldwin College in 1994 with a major in English.

A TOAST TO THE FUTURE

by Nora Egan

[Reprinted with permission from the Summer/Fall, 1992 issue of the *Global Nomad Quarterly*.]

Suddenly it came out, blurting like a geyser from the ground: I am a global nomad. Nothing has felt the same since.

I now have a culture. After three decades of learning other peoples' cultures, and still being an outsider, I look to the future. I see what is possible and work toward it. I am not bound by the past, though I am fascinated by it. I use it to prepare for the future, to take with me that which is useful for the journey. I do not hold on to the old ways just because I know them. I am future going. This is the way of my culture.

I no longer have to embody someone else's culture. I have paid my dues, trying to be French, then Italian, then USAmerican, then Chinese. Now I have found my own culture.

For many this would not be much of a revelation. They live as they are, and are comfortable with what they believe and how they behave. They can easily express an opinion, because they believe what they think, and trust they are right.

I have always been adjusting my feelings and perceptions, changing them and hiding them. I come by my convictions with the greatest of effort for I have lived in many places, living among different peoples, learning different languages. So for every opinion I might have come by naturally, there has always been another one, one backed by a culture and tradition. How, then, could I hold a conviction, other than one of multiple viewpoints? And if I were opinionated, I risked being alone. Since I was always a stranger knowing no one, my survival was my ability to fit in.

There are many feelings which have been difficult to balance as the result of this mobility and multicultural life, but especially the sense of being an outsider is reinforced daily, with silences after my multinational stories, and my not having the same references. How grateful I am for the chance encounters with other global nomads or transculturals, where the bond is frequently an electric one. Someone who understands and responds.

Although the experiences of each global nomad is different, we have a common experience of being outsiders. We have worked our way into being insiders through differences of language, culture, religion, class and personality, only to be pulled out again, to start over, and over, and over. The losses get suspended in the excitement of moving, only to balloon into a deep feeling of emptiness when the moving stops. It hurts to leave a life behind, even when it feels so exciting to be on a plane again.

The recognition has been life changing. For me, it is as if 3/4 of my life has emerged from shadow into full color. By telling, and having friends listen and acknowledge the losses and the findings, I have come to own them with pride. I reestablish in my present a legacy from my past that gives depth, and color, and history. I free myself from needing affirmation of my internationalness from the people in my day to day life, because I get that recognition from our group. I know that I belong, and that my ways are valid ways for global nomads. What a gift it is to have been given a name, and with it a whole community and culture.

So let me raise a toast to Global Nomads International, and to global nomads everywhere. We have seen the world, and know how much there is to do. Let us wait no longer to find others like ourselves, to give encouragement and get acknowledgement, and to begin making our mark on the world. Let our lives be filled with discussion, for it is by talking that we learn from others and pass our experiences on. Let us be aware of what happens with frequent change, so that our children may benefit from what we have learned, and our parents before us.

This is not to spare them one second of the loss or the renewal, but to acknowledge and affirm it, and to show guidance.

Here is to our future, and to the courage to make it what we need it to be.

Nora Egan, U.S. American-born global nomad, grew up in seven countries around the Mediterranean. Ms. Egan wrote "A Toast to the Future" in December 1991.

ADDITIONAL RESOURCES

Austin, Clyde N. *Cross-Cultural Reentry: A Book of Readings.* Abilene, Texas: Abilene Christian University, 1986.

> A collection of some of the best articles on reentry that pinpoint the problems and identify strategies for curing reverse culture shock.

Austin, Clyde N. *Cross-Cultural Reentry: An Annotated Bibliography.* Abilene, Texas: Abilene Christian University, 1983.

> A guided review of recent literature on cross-cultural reentry. A wonderful resource for anyone doing research on reentry issues.

Austin, Clyde N. *Descriptive Statements of Missionary Families.* Abilene, Texas: Clyde N. Austin, 1986.

> A telling "short-list" of characteristics of missionary families, differentiating them from other U.S. expatriate families.

Bettelheim, Bruno. *A Good Enough Parent: A Book on Childrearing.* New York: Alfred A. Knopf, 1987.

> Founded on the belief that parents must use their individual experience and creativity to parent successfully, this book covers many parenting dilemmas, including: the question "why," achieving identity, winning and losing, and the "real" Santa Claus.

Carris, Joan. *Hedgehogs in the Closet.* New York: J. B. Lippincott, 1988.

> This children's book compares U.S. customs, traditions and ways to the English (including differences of language) from the perspective of a child. It also explores some of the differences between going to a local English school and going to an international school.

Dean, Timothy. *Global Nomads -- Return to the Stone Age.* Vancouver, British Columbia, Canada: Action Now! Productions, Inc.

> Timothy Dean's videotape account of his global nomad childhood and his return to the Ukarumpa Village, where Dean grew up and where his father established a mission.

Eakin, Kay Branaman. *The Foreign Service Teenager -- At Home in the U.S.: A Few Thoughts for Parents Returning with Teenagers.* Washington, D.C.: Overseas Briefing Center/Foreign Service Institute, Department of State, 1988.

Focused on the special concerns of teens returning to the U.S. after living abroad, this booklet outlines many of the issues teens and their parents face and provides planning tools and suggestions for easing the adjustment.

Fritz, Jean. *Homesick: My Own Story.* New York: Dell Yearling, 1984.

This children's book tells the fictionalized story of Jean Fritz's own childhood experience as an MK in China. Set in 1925-1927, the story shares Jean's emotions as she moves from a turbulent China to peaceful Pennsylvania. This book also discusses Jean's feelings and expectations of the U.S., as someone who had never visited the U.S. before.

Galinsky, Ellen. *The Six Stages of Parenthood.* Reading, Massachusetts: Addison-Wesley Publishing Company, Inc., 1987.

This text identifies and explains the "life cycle" of parenting and provides suggestions for parents at each stage (image-making stage, nurturing stage, authority stage, interpretive stage, interdependent stage, and departure stage).

Gerner, Michael et al. "Characteristics of Internationally Mobile Adolescents." *Journal of School Psychology (Volume 30).* 1992.

Summarizes results of survey of over one thousand adolescent "third culture kids" by overseas school psychologists.

Giardini, Alyson M. *The Formation of a National Identity Among U.S. Citizens Growing Up Overseas.* Masters Degree Thesis, Stanford University, Winter, 1993.

Seen through the eyes of an American global nomad, this paper challenges traditional notions of personal identity as homogeneous and nation as bounded to a specific land.

Global Nomads: Cultural Bridges for the Future. Ithaca, New York: video produced by Alice Wu, Lewis Clark, Marianne Bøjer, and Illan Barzilay, Cornell University, 1994.

On this videotape, sixteen Cornell University students, four researchers and three university administrators give their impressions of the benefits and challenges of an internationally mobile lifestyle.

Going International: Beyond Culture Shock. San Francisco, CA: Griggs Productions, Inc., 1983.

Part of the *Going International* videotape series, this videotape is designed specifically for the family or individual moving abroad. Documentary style with feedback from real families and children.

Going International: Welcome Home, Stranger. San Francisco, CA: Griggs Productions, Inc., 1983.

Part of the *Going International* videotape series, this videotape focuses on the unexpected problems of returning home. Families share how they overcame the difficulties of "reentry."

Greenspan, Stanley. *The Essential Partnership: How Parents and Children Can Meet the Emotional Challenges of Infancy and Childhood.* New York: Viking Penguin, Inc., 1990.

Dr. Greenspan provides practical advice to parents on how to make a real emotional connection with their children, covering such problems as assertiveness and aggression, sexuality and pleasure, sadness and loss, self-esteem and confidence, competitiveness, fears, and more, as they relate to the development of children from infancy to age five.

Kalb, Rosalind and Welch, Penelope. *Moving Your Family Overseas.* Yarmouth, Maine: Intercultural Press, Inc., 1992.

This text covers every step of the move process including "breaking the news" to children, friends and relatives, the early days, making the most of home leave, parenting overseas, and moving on...moving home, among others.

Kohls, L. Robert. *Survival Kit for Overseas Living, Second Edition.* Yarmouth, Maine: Intercultural Press, Inc., 1984.

Bob Kohls' classic text on cross-cultural adjustments, this readable book covers concepts of culture, the ugly American, Rx for culture shock, intercultural communication, and more.

Let's Get a Move On! Newton, Massachusetts: KIDVIDZ, Inc.

> A videotape for children aged 4 - 10. Shows children sharing their feelings, getting ready, enjoying the adventure of a move, settling in and finding ways to make friends.

Main, Frank. *Perfect Parenting and Other Myths.* Minneapolis: CompCare Publications, 1986.

> A very readable, practical guide for mortals, based on the belief that The Brady Bunch and The Waltons were made for TV, not for real life. Includes sections on discipline, pitfalls of parenting extremes, sibling warfare, and perils of the single parent, among others.

McNichol, Tom. "The Wanderers." *In Health.* July/August 1991.

> Short essay on the experiences of a third culture kid. Includes tips from David Pollock.

Meltzer, Gail and Grandjean, Elaine. *The Moving Experience: A Practical Guide to Psychological Survival.* Philadelphia, Pennsylvania: Multilingual Matters Ltd., 1989.

> The authors highlight issues families and individuals face when moving. Topics include: staying put or just passing through, on foreign soil, the movable marriage, employment options, and the portable child.

Mitchell, Barbara. *Between Two Worlds: A Story about Pearl Buck.* Minneapolis, Minnesota: Carolrhoda Books, 1988.

> Encouraging, insightful and very easy to read, this book highlights how extraordinary Pearl Buck was. The author aptly describes Pearl Buck's ability to integrate her two worlds and to continuously relate to both of them.

Osborne, Philip. *Parenting for the '90s.* Intercourse, Pennsylvania: Good Books, 1989.

> A scholarly approach that puts into context many popular parenting theories and advances alternative strategies. Based on Osborne's concept of four problem areas (no problem, child's problem, parent's problem, and mutual problem).

Pascoe, Robin. *Culture Shock! Successful Living Abroad -- A Parent's Guide.* Singapore: Time Books International, 1994.

> Focuses on the emotional impact of a move on children. Includes chapters on Third Culture Kids, international schools, family culture shock, traveling with children, health and safety issues, and reentry.

Pascoe, Robin. *The Wife's Guide to Successful Living Abroad.* Singapore: Time Books International, 1992.

> This tongue-in-cheek, humorous text offers practical advice on how to handle pre-moving day jitters, the arrival, cultural transitions, portable careers, household help overseas, entertaining, home leave, and return shock.

Pollock, David C. *The Transition Model.* Albany, NY: Interaction, Inc., 1990.

> Audiocassette in which David Pollock discusses culture shock, the process of transition, and keys to making the transition successful. Also available on videotape.

Raising Children Abroad. Washington, D.C.: Produced by the Department of State's Family Liaison Office, Office of Overseas Schools, and Office of Security Awareness, 1993.

> Videotape coverage of behavioral changes associated with international moves, as well as issues of continuity, routine, rituals, national identity, security, adolescents, and more. Available to U.S. Foreign Affairs agencies and to Office of Overseas Schools-assisted institutions abroad.

Rigamer, E.F. "Stresses of Families Abroad." *Travel Medicine International.* London: 1985.

> A short essay on how overseas postings may cause stress to children and parents. Includes information on terrorism, family stress, adaptation, the role of the physician and psychiatrist, and prevention.

Romano, Dugan. *Intercultural Marriage: Promises and Pitfalls.* Yarmouth, Maine: Intercultural Press, 1988.

> A book focused on the needs of intercultural couples and families

that identifies 18 'troublespots' not as severe in monocultural marriages.

Shiff, Eileen. *Experts Advise Parents: A Guide to Raising Loving, Responsible Children.* New York: Delacorte Press, 1987.

A "parenting course in print," this text pulls together writings by some of the most respected child-rearing authorities of our times. Topics covered include: self-esteem, parents as teachers, discipline, responsibility, sexuality, and explaining death and divorce, *inter alia.*

Smith, Carolyn D. *The Absentee American: Repatriates' Perspectives on America.* Bayside, New York: Aletheia Publications, 1994.

Written by an absentee American, this book outlines the ordeals of Americans who lived outside their own country for a portion of their childhood and who have returned, with an emphasis on the long-term influence on the repatriated American's perspective of the U.S. and its place in the contemporary world.

Steinglass, Peter and Edwards, Martha E. *Family Relocation Study: Final Report.* New York: Ackerman Institute for Family Therapy for the U.S. Department of State, 1993.

Called the "Ackerman Study," this document reports the results of a study of State Department families with children, focusing on the effects of relocation on employee, spouse and children, on reentry issues, and on the impact of individual, social and relocation event factors on adjustment.

Teen Talk: Straight Talk About Moving... One Teen to Another. Franklin, Michigan: Conquest Corporation, 1993 Edition.

Marvelous tips from teens to teens, covering such issues as relationships with parents, making new friends, school (the first day and later on), and more.

Van Reken, Ruth. *Letters Never Sent.* Elgin, Illinois: David C. Cook Publishing Company, 1988.

Moving and cathartic, these letters recount the emotions and experience of an American woman growing up in a missionary family in Africa.

Ward, Ted. *Living Overseas: A Book of Preparations.* New York: The Free Press (a Division of Macmillan, Inc.), 1984.

This book offers details of what the overseas experience will offer and require, including chapters on your job and its context, planning the move, living with what you find, the skills of coping, and others.

Warschaw, Tessa Albert and Victoria Secunda. *Winning with Kids: How to Negotiate with Your Baby Bully, Kid Tyrant, Loner, Saint, Underdog or Winner So They Love Themselves and You, Too.* New York: Bantam Books, 1988.

Authors Warschaw and Secunda focus on negotiating skills as a method to resolve conflicts between parents and children, covering issues of style (parenting styles, children's styles), strategies of negotiation, negotiating with preschool and elementary school age youngsters, and negotiating with teenagers.

Wertsch, Mary Edwards. *Military Brats: Legacies of Childhood Inside the Fortress.* New York: Harmony Books, 1991.

Based on five years of research, Wertsch explores the long-term psychological effects of growing up amidst the moves and expectations of the military.

Williams, Karen Lynn. *When Africa Was Home.* New York: Orchard Books, 1991.

Fictionalized, picture book for children that deals with issues such as the Chichewa language, life in Africa, comparisons of a white child to a black child, animals, and the longing for Africa that Peter feels when he is back in the U.S.

Wood, David et al. "Impact of Family Relocation on Children's Growth, Development, School Function, and Behavior." *Journal of the American Medical Association.* Vol. 270, #11. September 15, 1993.

A depressing look at the impact of U.S. domestic moves on the development of children, with statistical findings on the impact of moves on school success and behavior.

ABOUT THE EDITOR

Karen Curnow McCluskey is founder and President of Global Training Associates, a Virginia-based consulting company providing management, diversity, and cross-cultural training services to a variety of corporate, government and academic organizations. Having lived and worked in France, Turkey, Kenya, and Austria, Ms. McCluskey has offered international training, human resource consulting, and writing support services for over 13 years. She earned her undergraduate degrees in Business Administration and French from the Sorbonne/University of Paris (Paris, France) and Houghton College (Houghton, New York) and her MBA in International Management and Marketing from U.S. International University (Nairobi, Kenya). Ms. McCluskey lives with her husband and two daughters in northern Virginia.